PSYCHOANALYTIC PSYCHOTHERAPY

IN THE

KLEINIAN TRADITION

Also edited by Sue Johnson & Stanley Ruszczynski
and published by Karnac Books:

PSYCHOANALYTIC PSYCHOTHERAPY IN THE INDEPENDENT TRADITION

PSYCHOANALYTIC PSYCHOTHERAPY

IN THE

KLEINIAN TRADITION

edited by

Stanley Ruszczynski & Sue Johnson

London
KARNAC BOOKS

First published in 1999 by
H. Karnac (Books) Ltd.
58 Gloucester Road
London SW7 4QY

British Library Cataloguing in Publication Data

A C.I.P. record for this book is available from the British Library.

ISBN 1-85575-175-5

Edited, designed, and produced by Communication Crafts

Printed in Great Britain by Polestar Wheatons Ltd, Exeter

10 9 8 7 6 5 4 3 2 1

for Stella, Jamie, and Helen,
and Mike

ACKNOWLEDGEMENTS

We would like to sincerely thank all the authors for their chapters, often written in holiday time, or in precious free time, or between patients, teaching commitments, and other professional activities, whilst also trying to live life! We would also like to thank them for bearing with us both in our pressurizing of them and in our long silences as we tried to get on with the editing. We hope that they will be as pleased as we are with the end result.

We are very grateful to Cesare Sacerdoti and Graham Sleight and their team at Karnac Books for patiently waiting for this book and its sister volume, *Psychoanalytic Psychotherapy in the Independent Tradition*, published at the same time. Cesare Sacerdoti's sensitive but realistic understanding and forbearance of the shortcomings of psychotherapists trying to write, edit, and publish and his commitment to this project encouraged and sustained us. We are also indebted to Klara and Eric King for their skilful part in the production of these books.

We would like to thank those friends and colleagues who encouraged us and shared our excitement, and especially Faith Miles, who was particularly helpful in assisting us. We would like to acknowledge the British Association of Psychotherapists, which trained us and which makes up an important part of our professional lives. We are especially grateful to our personal psychoanalysts and to those who supervised our clinical work during our training.

An earlier version of Philip Roys's chapter was published in *Reconstructing Infancy, Monograph No. 7, British Association of Psychotherapists*, 1996, under the title, "Reconstructing Infancy— A Kleinian View", and parts of it were published in the *Oxford Psychotherapy Society Bulletin, No. 26*, November, 1997.

On behalf of the contributors to this volume, we thank all of our patients, without whom this book could not have been written. We have made every effort to disguise clinical material so as to ensure anonymity and to use only that that is absolutely necessary for purposes of illustration. Through writing this book, the authors want to describe to colleagues their way of thinking about their clinical experiences. The purpose of this is to go on learning through developing theoretical understanding of, and therefore clinical work with, those people who come to our consulting-rooms.

CONTENTS

ix

CONTRIBUTORS

MARY ADAMS is an Associate Member of the British Association of Psychotherapists and has a full-time private practice of psychoanalytic psychotherapy. She is a member of the editorial board of the *Journal of the British Association of Psychotherapists*. She has published in psychotherapy journals.

JEAN ARUNDALE is a Full Member of and Training Therapist for the British Association of Psychotherapists and has a private practice of psychoanalytic psychotherapy. She is a Clinical Supervisor in the Psychology Department and at the York Clinic in Guy's Hospital, London, and teaches for the British Association of Psychotherapists and other psychotherapy trainings. She is the Editor of the *British Journal of Psychotherapy*.

NOEL HESS is a Full Member of the British Association of Psychotherapists and has a private practice of psychoanalytic psychotherapy. He works in the NHS as a Clinical Psychologist (Specialist in Psychoanalytic Psychotherapy) in the Department of Psychological Medicine and Psychotherapy, University College

Hospital, London. He is actively engaged in teaching for the British Association of Psychotherapists and other psychotherapy trainings. His publications and research interests include old age, depression, schizoid states, and the application of psychoanalytic thinking to theatre and film.

SUE JOHNSON is a Full Member of the British Association of Psychotherapists and has a full-time private practice of psycho-analytic psychotherapy and supervision. She had previously been employed part-time as a psychotherapist at the Brandon Centre for Counselling and Psychotherapy for Young People, London, where she worked with adolescents and their families. She teaches on a number of courses for the British Association of Psychotherapists.

EVELYN KATZ is a Full Member of the British Association of Psychotherapists and has a private practice of psychoanalytic psychotherapy and supervision. She works at the Student Counselling Service at King's College, University of London, providing psychotherapy for students and supervision to counsellors on placement. Previously she worked part-time as a psychotherapist at the Camden Psychotherapy Unit, London. She is involved in teaching for the British Association of Psychotherapists.

SUSAN LIPSHITZ-PHILLIPS is a Clinical Psychologist and an Adult Psychotherapist trained at the Tavistock Clinic. She is a Full Member of the British Association of Psychotherapists and has a private practice of psychoanalytic psychotherapy. She is actively engaged in postgraduate education within the British Association of Psychotherapists and is a Visiting Teacher at the Tavistock Clinic, London. Previously, she worked as a psychotherapist at the Camden Psychotherapy Unit, London, and has lectured on psychoanalytic theory at various universities and in South Africa. She has contributed to books and journals.

PHILIP ROYS is a Full Member of the British Association of Psychotherapists and has a private practice of psychoanalytic psychotherapy in Oxford. He is a member of the British Association of Psychotherapists' Psychoanalytic Training Committee. He is Co-ordinator of the Isis Centre (Oxfordshire Mental Healthcare NHS Trust) in Oxford, which provides a community-based counselling and psychotherapy service and offers training and consultation to NHS and other professionals.

STANLEY RUSZCZYNSKI is a Full Member of the British Association of Psychotherapists and has a private practice of psychoanalytic psychotherapy. He is a Principal Adult Psychotherapist at the Portman Clinic (Tavistock and Portman NHS Trust), London. He is a founder Member of the Society of Psychoanalytic Marital Psychotherapists and for a number of years was a senior member of staff in the Tavistock Marital Studies Institute (Tavistock Centre), London, serving as Deputy Director and both Clinical and Training Co-ordinator. He is the editor of *Psychotherapy with Couples* (Karnac Books, 1993), co-editor (with James Fisher) of *Intrusiveness and Intimacy in the Couple* (Karnac Books, 1995), and the author of a number of book chapters and journal papers. He undertakes clinical teaching for the British Association of Psychotherapists.

PSYCHOANALYTIC PSYCHOTHERAPY
IN THE
KLEINIAN TRADITION

Introduction

Stanley Ruszczynski & Sue Johnson

For the purposes of this volume, what is meant by the "Kleinian tradition" is that clinical and theoretical orientation initiated by Melanie Klein, following on the work of Freud, but significantly developed by, in particular, Wilfred Bion, Herbert Rosenfeld, and Hanna Segal, and more recently by, amongst others, Betty Joseph, John Steiner, and Ronald Britton. The development of this line of thought is well summarized by Elizabeth Bott Spillius (1988, 1994), and its major theoretical and clinical concepts are comprehensively described by Robert Hinshelwood (1989, 1994).

The central theoretical concepts that inform the work of those practising in the Kleinian tradition are that of unconscious phantasy (Isaacs, 1948; Klein, 1958), the paranoid–schizoid and the depressive positions (Klein, 1935, 1946), projective identification (Klein, 1946)—especially as it has been developed by Bion and Rosenfeld to be understood as a form of communication (Bion, 1959; Rosenfeld, 1971)—the centrality of the oedipal situation (Britton, 1992b, 1998; Britton, Feldman, & O'Shaughnessy, 1989) and the theory of the container and the contained (Bion, 1962).

1

There are other important theoretical constructs (see Hinshelwood, 1989), but those mentioned here are probably the most in-
fluential for psychoanalytic psychotherapists who work in the
Kleinian tradition.

It is relevant to note that these theoretical constructs bridge
into clinical practice and are not only theoretically central but also
help the clinician to think about the nature of the transference–
countertransference relationship, the analysis of which is at the
heart of contemporary psychoanalytic practice. Psychoanalysis
has always grown from a fertile interaction between theory and
clinical practice. Clinical experience comes to challenge the contemporary theoretical understanding and demands a development of that theoretical understanding so as to accommodate the
emerging clinical experiences.

A vivid illustration of this theoretical and clinical interplay is
the way in which Kleinian concepts—especially that of projective
identification (Klein, 1946)—were used in the late 1940s and 1950s
by clinicians such as Bion, Rosenfeld, and Segal to work psychoanalytically with borderline and psychotic patients, without significantly adapting their technique. As a result, there developed
the need for yet further theoretical understanding of the psychotic
parts of the personality. It soon became clear that this theoretical
development was necessary for understanding not only the more
severely disturbed patients, but also the more primitive aspects of
those patients who would not be so considered.

More recently, clinical experience with narcissistic and borderline patients has led to the development of the concept of
pathological organizations of the mind (Joseph, 1975, 1982;
O'Shaughnessy, 1981; Rosenfeld, 1964; Segal, 1972). Steiner uses
the evocative description of "psychic retreats" in his discussion of
this complex and rigid psychic structure, developed by certain
patients as a defence against both the fragmentation of the paranoid–schizoid position and the pain and mourning required by
the move towards the depressive position (Steiner, 1993). Such
psychic structures function defensively but also produce particular states of mind where, because the "bad" parts of the self are
in the ascendancy over the "good" parts, considerable relief and
pleasure is gained from pathological and perverse object relationships. This understanding of "negative narcissism" (Rosenfeld,

1971a) has proven to be extremely useful clinically with a broad range of patients who are often experienced as rigid, perverse, and difficult to treat. The concept has also been extremely useful in helping the understanding of very disturbed couples in psychoanalytic couple psychotherapy, who, on the basis of this rigid and pathological object-relating, established a near-impenetrable sado-masochistic relationship, which Mary Morgan has evocatively called a "gridlock" (Morgan, 1995). The theoretical value and clinical usefulness of this understanding of such pathological organizations of the mind is clearly demonstrated by the regularity with which many of the authors in this volume refer to it in their discussions.

Following on the work of Freud, who referred to the "abnormal ego" and "psychotic part" of every normal person (Freud, 1937), psychoanalytic psychotherapists influenced in their thinking by Klein have been very interested in the relationship between different parts of the personality. Klein's concepts of the paranoid–schizoid position and the depressive position have been central to thinking not only about different parts of the mind but also about how an individual will throughout life—including in the analytic relationship—oscillate between more and less mature aspects of their personality. This is especially important in following the details of the transference relationship as it is enacted in the therapeutic encounter. This understanding, together with an understanding of the process of projective identification both as a defensively evacuative process and as a means of unconscious communication, make up the heart of clinical practice. The container–contained conceptualization offers an understanding of the means whereby the psychoanalytic psychotherapist can play his or her part in the psychotherapeutic relationship (Bion, 1962b).

The chapters contained in this volume all, in their different ways, address these core concepts, as well as raising a number of others.

In Chapter 1, "Recollections and Historical Reconstruction", Philip Roys outlines the Kleinian understanding of infantile development and shows how this informs clinical practice with the adult patient in intensive treatment. He refers to many of the concepts that are further elaborated by the writers of the subsequent chapters. Roys reminds us that Klein's delineation of the paranoid–schizoid and depressive positions is a description of states of mind rather than of developmental stages, and he shows how the clinician may be able to observe and experience, in the transference–countertransference relationship, the way the patient constantly oscillates between these positions. Using detailed clinical material, Roys demonstrates how an analysis of the contemporary interaction between therapist and patient leads to the reconstruction, in the clinical encounter, of infantile anxieties and defences. He goes on to show how an understanding of these anxieties and defences leads to insight into the ways in which they inform the internal and external world of the patient.

In Chapter 2, "On the Persistence of Early Loss and Unresolved Mourning", Susan Lipshitz-Phillips takes up a similar theme by revisiting Freud's concept of the repetition compulsion (Freud, 1920g), especially in relation to the centrality of the experience of loss, in its many guises, and its influence on development. Lipshitz-Phillips shows how potent a force loss very often is, be it a loss such as that experienced on the birth of a sibling or the crippling premature loss of a mother. Using both clinical material and illustrations from literature she shows how various defensive arrangements can be made to ward off knowledge of the losses suffered. However, her argument is that in the transference relationship to the psychotherapist the residue of these unresolved losses will reappear and will need to be resolved so as to give the patient an opportunity to go on developing.

In these two chapters there is both implicit and explicit reference to the complex interaction between the internal world of the child and adult and the external reality within which they find themselves living their life.

In Chapter 3, "Interrelationships Between Internal and External Factors in Early Development: Current Kleinian Thinking and Implications for Technique", Jessica Sacret takes the reader to the heart of that which is often considered to be one of the central differences between psychoanalytic schools of thought: the place given to internal and external reality in the understanding of an individual's growth and development and current object relationships. She demonstrates how Kleinian thinking has developed, especially since Bion's seminal delineation of the containing function of the mother (Bion, 1962a, 1962b), to a clearer and more detailed picture of the complex dynamic interrelationship between the internal world and external reality. Using the particular situation of trauma, both in its more dramatic form such as disasters and gross abuse and in its more subtle form such as failed maternal containment, Sacret shows that pathological organizations of the mind may be constructed to defend the patient against the psychic impact of external realities as well as against the ravages of internal fears and phantasies. An attempt to understand the inevitable and intricate interrelationship between the two is central to Sacret's chapter.

Klein and those who followed after her put an emphasis on the ways in which the internal world, with its expectations and projections, significantly influences the perception of the external world. However, though this emphasis influences both theoretical understanding and clinical practice, Klein herself, as well as those who followed her, clearly included the reality of the external world in their understanding of the development of the infant mind and object relations. Klein described how, "an inner world is . . . built up in the child's unconscious mind, corresponding to his actual experiences and the impressions he gains from people and the external world, and yet altered by his own phantasies and impulses. If it is a world of people predominantly at peace with each other and with the ego, inner harmony, security and integration ensue" (Klein, 1940, p. 345–346). She goes on to add that "unpleasant experiences and the lack of enjoyable ones, in the young child, especially lack of happy and close contact with loved people, increase ambivalence, diminish trust and hope and confirm anxieties about inner annihilation and external persecution" (Klein, 1940, p. 347). In summary, she writes, "from its inception analysis has always laid stress on the importance of the child's early experiences, but it seems to me that only since we know more about the nature and contents of its early anxieties, and the continuous interplay between its actual experiences and its phantasy-life, can we fully understand *why* the external factor is so important" (Klein, 1935, p. 285).

In Chapter 4, "Turning a Blind Eye: Misrepresentation and the Denial of Life Events", Mary Adams describes the developmental struggle involved in coming to terms with certain "facts of life", namely dependence, the differences between the sexes and between the generations, and the inevitability of time and death (Money-Kyrle, 1968). She shows how these facts can be dealt with either by coming to tolerate them and so facing reality and diminishing narcissistic and omnipotent phantasies, or by misrepresenting them, specifically by lying to oneself. Using clinical material, she shows how misrepresentation may produce a form of delusional escape from facing the facts of life but how crippling to emotional growth such a defensive construction is likely to be. This understanding of how such perverse states of mind can develop is central to informing clinical work with many different types of patients.

In Chapter 5, "Tolerating Emotional Knowledge", Stanley Ruszczynski discusses the process of containment and locates its development in the experience of the nature of the relationship to, and resolution of, the oedipal situation. He shows how coming to tolerate the truly triangular nature of the oedipal situation is essential in developing the capacity for containment. This requires the mourning of the loss of the phantasied sole possession of the mother or the father, and coming to tolerate the special link between the parents (Britton, 1989). He argues that containment requires both receptivity and reflection on the part of the psychoanalytic psychotherapist, capacities analogous to those that might be considered to be respectively the female and the male functions. It is when the two can be allowed to come together that there will most probably be an opportunity for understanding and hence development and growth. Britton has recently delineated this by differentiating between what he calls subjective and objective awareness of experience. He shows how either form of awareness, alone, will be partial and defensive, but that the capacity to tolerate both will lead to knowledge, both of the self and of the other (Britton, 1998).

The next two chapters address particular pathological conditions, some form of which is likely to be familiar to most clinicians in their daily practice, namely that of depression and perversion (in this case, paedophilia).

In Chapter 6, "Psychoanalytic Psychotherapy for Chronic Depression", Noel Hess addresses what he suggests is the most common complaint presented by patients, and he goes on to suggest that what patients refer to as "depression" is likely to cover a variety of underlying pathologies with a spectrum of severities. His chapter is a detailed exploration of intensive psychoanalytic psychotherapy with a patient who presents with a chronic condition, where the depression has infiltrated the structure of the personality, rather than being a more acute presentation of a depressive episode in a previously reasonably well-functioning person. Touching on some of the ideas also discussed by Susan Lipshitz-Phillips in Chapter 2, Hess refers to the centrality of the experience of loss and the mourning required as part of its resolution. He shows how these are common to all forms of depression, whatever the degree of severity. He discusses both Freud's and Klein's seminal writings on melancholia and mourning (Freud, 1917e; Klein, 1935, 1940) and, following Klein, argues that mourning in adult life unconsciously reawakens infantile losses in relation to the primary maternal figure and all her functions. How this loss of the internal mother has been dealt with during the course of normal development will determine the process of mourning following a real external loss in adulthood.

In Chapter 7, "Notes on a Case of Paedophilia", Jean Arundale gives a vivid and detailed account of psychoanalytic psychotherapy with a severely disturbed patient who presented himself for treatment disturbed by the fact that he regularly entertained fantasies of sexual activity with underage males. The aggression at the heart of all perverse fantasy and activity became central to the therapeutic work with this patient, and Arundale clearly illustrates Stoller's, and others', understanding of sexual perversions being the "erotic form of hatred" (Stoller, 1976). As the clinical work developed with this patient, the despair and desolation often underlying such pathology began to emerge and become available for treatment.

In the final chapter, Chapter 8, "When Is Enough Enough? The Process of Termination with an Older Patient", Evelyn Katz discusses the process of termination, both in general—all psychotherapeutic treatments come to an end, be it planned or precipitate and premature—but specifically, in detail, termination with an older patient. She suggests that termination with this group of patients might have particular implications, and she reviews the literature on criteria for ending treatment as part of her discussion. She shows, however, that the capacity for more realistic and therefore depressive functioning continues to be the aim of the psychotherapeutic treatment of all patients, whatever stage of life they might have reached.

All the chapters in this volume address the individual patient's struggle to come to know and tolerate some of the indisputable facts of life, including dependency, the double difference between the sexes and between the generations, the true nature of the triangle of the oedipal situation, the life-long oscillations between the paranoid–schizoid and the depressive states of mind, and the inevitability of loss. It is indisputable that there is often a range of internal forces organized in order that this knowledge be evaded, and it is, therefore, necessary for this internal saboteur to come to be known as well. This illustrates Bion's view that "knowledge" is the third factor of psychic life, alongside those of "love" and "hate". Freud had already alerted us to this in one of his final papers, "Analysis Terminable and Interminable", where he writes that, "we must not forget that the analytic relationship is based on a love of truth—that is, a recognition of reality—and that it precludes any kind of sham or deceit" (Freud, 1937c). This recognition of emotional reality, the gaining of knowledge and insight, has always been a central aim of the psychotherapeutic practice of psychoanalysis. The writers of the following chapters show how they go about promoting this in their daily clinical practice.

CHAPTER ONE

Recollection and historical reconstruction

Philip Roys

Writing in 1937, Freud commented that "the work of analysis aims at inducing the patient to give up the repressions . . . belonging to his early development and to replace them with reactions of a sort that would correspond to a psychically mature condition. With this purpose in view, he must be brought to recollect certain experiences and the affective impulses up called by them which he has for the time being forgotten" (Freud, 1937, pp. 257–258).

That such recollection is central to psychoanalytic psychotherapy there can be no dispute, but there are different points of view about what precisely might be recalled and how this should be achieved; in particular, historical reconstruction tends to be approached differently by contemporary Kleinians and those of other orientations.

In this chapter, I intend to explore contemporary Kleinian technique in psychoanalytic psychotherapy, with particular reference to the question of historical reconstruction. I shall suggest that it is possible to delineate a distinctively Kleinian approach to historical reconstruction which follows from the Kleinian account of the development of mind and of its functioning.

Kleinian thought seems to have acquired the reputation of being difficult to understand. In part, this may result from the fact that much of its concern is with primitive experience that, by its very nature, is remote from adult experience and thought. But I think that, in addition to this, there may be something in the nature of the account that is provided—a dynamic, constantly moving picture—which can make it complex and troubling. I shall, therefore, begin by attempting to clarify some basic concepts, in the hope that this will facilitate clearer understanding of what follows.

Unconscious phantasy

A central concern of Kleinians is with the internal world. Melanie Klein "created a revolutionary addition to the model of the mind; namely, that we do not live in one world but in two—that we live in an internal world which is as real a place to live as the outside world" (Meltzer, 1981, p. 178).

Now, the important point here is not that as an outside observer it is possible to describe the contents of the mind of another objectively, but that we all have an awareness (albeit unconscious) of important things going on inside us.

At the deepest level of the mind, this awareness exists as unconscious phantasy. "An unconscious phantasy is a belief in the activity of concretely felt 'internal' objects" (Hinshelwood, 1989, p. 34). Hinshelwood provides a clear illustration: Take, for example, the infant who is hungry. His bodily sensations given by his physiology are also experienced subjectively and psychologically. The discomfort is attributed to the motivation of a malevolent object actually located in his tummy that intends to cause the discomfort of hunger. A *good* internal object is experienced when the infant is fed and feels the warm milk giving satisfying sensations in his tummy (Hinshelwood, 1989, pp. 34–35).

The concept of unconscious phantasy, then, "being the mental representation of instinctual impulses is the nearest psychological phenomenon to the biological nature of the human being" (Hinshelwood, 1989, p. 34) and thus provides a link between biology and psychology. At the most primitive levels, unconscious phantasy is experienced by the individual in terms of objects that are felt to be concrete (as having a real existence inside or outside) and are believed to have good and bad motivations (towards the subject).

But there is much more to unconscious phantasy than the recognition of good and bad objects. "In the mental development of the infant . . . phantasy soon becomes also a means of defence against anxieties, a means of inhibiting and controlling instinctual urges and an expression of negative wishes as well" (Isaacs, 1952, p. 83).

Over time, this phantasy world of objects and of the relationships between them develops. "Growth and evolution of an individual are due not only to physiological growth and the maturation of the perceptual apparatus—memory, and so on—but also to accumulated experience and learning from reality. Learning from reality is, in turn, connected with the evolution and changes in phantasy life. Phantasies evolve. There is a constant struggle between the infant's omnipotent phantasies and the encounter of realities, good and bad" (Segal, 1991, p. 26).

In many ways, the concept of the internal world with its unconscious phantasy life and objects is rather mysterious and difficult to grasp. Everyday expressions such as being "gnawed by hunger" or having "butterflies in the tummy" may be suggestive of an internal world of live objects, but in themselves these expressions are probably not convincing.

The evidence for the existence of this world of phantasy came initially from Melanie Klein's play technique, in which the play of a child was regarded in the same way as the free associations of the adult in analysis—that is, as demonstrating the unconscious phantasies active in the patient's mind.

Klein says:

Take, for instance, the case of Ruth who, as an infant, had gone hungry for some time because her mother had little milk to give her. At the age of four years and three months, when playing with the wash basin, she called the water tap a milk tap. She declared that the milk was running into mouths (the holes in the waste pipe), but that only a very little was flowing. This unsatisfied oral desire made its appearance in countless games and dramatizations and showed itself in her whole attitude. For instance, she asserted that she was poor, that she only had one coat and that she had very little to eat—none of these statements being in the least in accordance with reality. [Klein, 1926, pp. 135–136]

But it is a long way from the unconscious phantasy life of the infant to that of the adult. It is to the development of the individual and the interaction between internal and external worlds that I now wish to turn.

The concept of position

In contrast to Freud, Klein held that from birth the infant has a rudimentary ego that experiences anxiety and takes measures to deal with this. This primitive ego utilizes defence mechanisms and forms internal and external object relations.

In considering the question of the development of the infant, Melanie Klein eventually moved away from Freud's scheme of libidinal stages (oral, anal, genital, etc.) and utilized instead a model that, via the concept of "position", emphasized the fluctuations and the dynamic quality of psychic functioning and development. The term "position" refers to a particular constellation of impulses, anxieties, and defences. Melanie Klein described two positions: the paranoid–schizoid and the depressive. These refer to two types of anxieties and the characteristic defences and object relationships that the ego employs to deal with these.

In one sense, these two positions could be seen as phases of development, the paranoid–schizoid position occupying the first three to four months of the infant's life and gradually being superseded by the depressive position. But this would be very misleading, for the depressive position never completely replaces the paranoid–schizoid position. As Segal argues: "the integration achieved is never complete, and defences against the depressive conflict bring about regression to paranoid–schizoid phenomena, so that the individual at all times may oscillate between the two" (Segal, 1964, p. ix).

In utilizing the concept of position, therefore, Klein was not just describing infantile development; she was outlining two characteristic groups of anxieties and defences that persist throughout life. There is "a continuous movement between the two positions . . . so that neither dominates with any degree of completeness or permanence . . . we observe periods of integration leading to the depressive position functioning or disintegration and fragmentation resulting in a paranoid–schizoid state" (Steiner, 1992, p. 48).

What, then, are the characteristics of these positions, which form such an important part of the Kleinian model of the mind?

The paranoid–schizoid position

The paranoid–schizoid position refers to a group of anxieties and defences associated with an immature ego preoccupied with the question of its own survival. The infant is assailed by anxieties from within and without, which are felt to threaten its very existence. These anxieties and defences are experienced in terms of concrete unconscious phantasies such as those described above.

The immature ego takes steps to rid itself of bad experiences and to maintain good experiences by splitting itself and its objects into two parts, good and bad. The bad experience is projected outwards. But although the infant may have succeeded in diminishing a bad and threatening *internal* experience, a price has been paid. It is now faced with a persecuting *external* object as well as with whatever is felt to remain of the bad internal experience. This is the prototype of the persecuting object relationship.

At the same time, in an effort to foster good experiences, good parts of the self are projected to create an ideal object relationship.

The separation of good from bad and the desperate attempt to hold on to the good and get rid of the bad is one of the characteristic features of paranoid–schizoid functioning. The central anxiety is paranoid—a fear of being attacked and overwhelmed by hostile internal and external forces. The primitive defences employed to deal with this (splitting, projective identification, and idealization) aim to keep the bad as far away as possible from the good. But although moments of idealization may be created, the sense of persecution will be in the background, ready at any moment to return to centre stage.

The paranoid–schizoid position is, then, characterized by a desperate struggle for survival and the complex phantasy world that is elaborated as the infant deals with primitive anxieties.

The external world

So far, the focus has been on the phantasies that the infant has about its impulses and objects and of its relationships with them. But what of the real external world? Does this have any impact, or, as is sometimes suggested, does the external environment have little significance in Kleinian thinking?

While it is certainly the case that a major preoccupation is with the internal world, it would be misleading to conclude that the external world has no importance in Kleinian thought. Rather, it is suggested that there is an interaction between the two, with the state of the internal world affecting the perception of the external world, but with the real external world shaping the state of the internal world. Thus, phantasies, which are projected, can either be confirmed and reinforced by the external world, or the external world can lead to their modification. Cycles of projection and introjection can move in a negative or in a positive direction.

To take a simple illustration, let us return to the example of the hungry infant. In an attempt to deal with the bad object felt to be inside him, he will tend to project this outside. He will then be faced with a persecuting outside world.

This begins a process, the outcome of which will depend upon the strength of the infant's rage and the qualities of the real object (in this case, the breast) in terms of its capacity to satisfy his hunger. If the infant's rage is not too great and the mother responds sensitively and soon enough, the bad object felt to be attacking the infant will be modified by the good object that has been presented to him. His phantasy will be changed in a positive direction.

If, however, his rage and therefore his persecutory phantasies are very strong and/or his mother fails to respond in time, then the outside world will tend to confirm his internal phantasies. The perception of a bad and persecuting world will be perpetuated. The screaming, hungry infant who turns away when the breast is offered may be seen as having had his persecutory phantasies reinforced. He has been faced with a breast that is terrifying rather than a good object capable of satisfying his needs.

The illustration above enormously oversimplifies the phantasy life of the infant and his efforts to deal with internal anxieties, instinctual urges, and the frustrations of external reality. What I hope it does convey, however, is something of the complicated interaction between internal phantasy and the external world, of how phantasy colours the perception of reality, and of how reality can lead either to its modification or to its reinforcement and confirmation.

The depressive position

How, then, does the infant move forward from the paranoid–schizoid position? The key issue is whether good experiences have sufficiently outweighed bad experiences. Under favourable internal and external conditions, at the age of about four to five months, the infant will gradually become convinced of the resilience of his good object and his libidinal impulses in the face of his bad object and his destructive impulses. There will therefore be less need to project bad parts outside, and the external world will therefore be less dangerous and persecuting. With a more benign internal and external environment, the need to split and project diminishes, resulting in a push towards integration.

The infant is now at the frontier of the depressive position, in which he comes to recognize that the same object that is capable of meeting his needs and wishes can also frustrate them and that he can feel both love and hate towards it. "This is not simply an enlargement of awareness and knowledge, but the disruption of the existing psychic world of the infant. What had previously been separate worlds of timeless bliss in one ideal universe of experience, and terror and persecution in another alternative universe, now turn out to be one world. And they come, these contrasting experiences, from one source . . ." (Britton, 1992b, pp. 38–39).

In the depressive position, there is a shift from concern about the survival of the self to include concern for the internal and external good object. Feelings of guilt and of genuine concern for the object (and not merely for the gratification that it gives), if tolerable and tolerated, lead to a hope that all might not be lost after all, that some repair or reparation might be possible. "This is based on the sense of an internal world in which some goodness survives, whatever paroxysm of bad feelings sweep across it" (Hinshelwood, 1989, p. 148).

The working-through of the depressive position represents a major developmental milestone. If the painful "sense of distinction between self and object and between the real and the ideal object" (Britton, 1992b, p. 40) can be borne, the infant gradually enters a psychic universe in which he is able to accept reality (which can be painful and frustrating) and engage in symbolic thinking.

But the intense conflict engendered in the depressive position may be too much to bear. In this case, the experiences that cannot be faced will be avoided. Briefly, there are two main groups of defences that might be called upon—paranoid and manic. The use of paranoid defences involves a retreat from the threshold of the depressive position back to the paranoid–schizoid position. The reinstitution of splitting and projective identification and other primitive defences ensures that good and bad are separated, omnipotent control is maintained, and depressive reality and its associated anxiety and conflicts are thereby avoided.

Manic defences are a particular group of primitive defences distinguished by their aim of denying depressive anxiety and guilt. "In this state the source of conflict is that the ego is unwilling and unable to renounce its good internal objects and yet endeavours to escape from the perils of dependence on them as well as from its bad objects and id" (Klein, 1935, p. 227). Segal argues that "the manic relation is characterized by a triad of feelings . . . control, triumph and contempt" (Segal, 1964, p. 83).

With the advent of the depressive position, there is the possibility of love and goodness becoming integrated with and prevailing over hate and badness. There is a question, however, of whether this love and goodness will survive the knowledge of the Oedipus situation. Britton suggests that "just as in the depressive position the idea of permanent possession has to be given up, so in confronting the parental relationship the idea of one's sole possession of the desired parent has to be relinquished" (Britton, 1992b, p. 40).

For some, however, relinquishing the idea of being the special one proves impossible, and "life, instead of being lived, can become the vehicle for the reinstatement of ... defensive illusions, and the relationships of the external world are used only as stage props for an insistent internal drama whose function is to deny the psychic reality of the depressive position and the real Oedipus situation" (Britton, 1992, p. 45).

Kleinian technique

What, then, are the implications of the above point of view for therapeutic technique?

Specifically, it is the view of unconscious phantasy, and of how this infuses the transference, which informs Kleinian technique and tends to distinguish it from other approaches. Hinshelwood, for example, suggests that the transference " ... is not ... merely a repetition of old attitudes, events and traumas from the past, it is an externalization of unconscious phantasy 'here-and-now'" (Hinshelwood, 1989, p. 15).

According to this view, the "experiences and the affective impulses" (Freud, 1937d, p. 258), which have been forgotten and must be recalled, are not just patterns of relating to key figures or important incidents from the past, but the internal world of the patient as manifested in his *total* attitude to the therapist and the therapeutic situation.

Other approaches tend to view the transference and the therapeutic task differently. Ponsi comments: "In the classical conception, since the analyst assumed that an event was being repeated, he focused his attention as reconstruction of the infantile history, with a view to freeing the patient thereby from the restrictions of the repetition compulsion" (Ponsi, 1997, p. 243).

A succinct illustration is given by Freud:

> One lays before the subject of the analysis a piece of his early history that he has forgotten, in some such way as this: "Up to your Nth year you regarded yourself as the sole and unlimited possessor of your mother, then came another baby and brought you grave disillusionment. Your mother left you for some time, and even after she reappeared she was never again devoted to you exclusively. Your feelings towards your mother became ambivalent, your father gained a new importance for you" . . . and so on. [Freud, 1937d, p. 261]

There have been many developments in psychoanalytic theory and technique since 1937, but to the extent that the transference is still conceived of as the repetition of *events*, this leads to an emphasis on the patient being freed from the repetition compulsion by means of historical reconstruction. Thus, a contemporary Freudian, Sharon Raeburn, comments that "reconstructions are still an important part of psychoanalytic therapy, because repressed early experiences are highly emotionally charged and are repeated in actions" (Raeburn, 1996, p. 6).

The Kleinian view is somewhat different:

> unconscious phantasy, the cause of the transference is not something that occasionally irrupts into the patient's relation with the analyst and then interferes with his reason and Cupertino. It is the fertile matrix from which his actual motives spring and which determine his apparently rational behaviour—no less than his silence and negation and openly defiant resistance. The therapeutic task of extending the patient's knowledge about himself, about his unconscious impulses and defences against anxiety and pain, makes it necessary to bring his unconscious phantasies to consciousness. [Heimann, 1956, p. 113]

According to the Kleinian view, therefore, it is the task of the therapist to explicate the unconscious phantasies that the patient brings to the consulting-room. It is the refusal of the therapist to fit in with these unconscious phantasies that is a key factor in promoting change. By his interpretations, the therapist explicates the patient's underlying unconscious phantasies; if effective, these interpretations will reduce the patient's distortions of the therapist, which result from his unconscious phantasies. This creates the possibility of the internalization of new object relationships in a changed internal world.

Fairbairn eloquently summarizes this view:

> Psychoanalytic treatment resolves itself into a struggle on the part of the patient to press-gang his relationship with the analyst into the closed system of the inner world through the agency of the transference and a determination on the part of the analyst to effect a breach in this closed system. . . . [Fairbairn, 1958, p. 385]

Projective identification

The concept of projective identification describes the process whereby the patient tries to "press-gang" (Fairbairn, 1958, p. 385) his relationship with the therapist to fit in with his unconscious phantasies. The concept refers to the process by which parts of the self are, in phantasy, split off and projected into another object. The "projector", in phantasy, thereby changes the object, which now contains the projected part. There are a number of possible motives for so doing—for example, to control the object, to avoid separation, to evacuate a bad quality.

A question of some interest and controversy has been the extent to which this process is merely a phantasy in the mind of the projector and the extent to which the recipient of the projection can be changed to conform to the projector's unconscious phantasy. Bion, for example, suggested that projective identification, as well as operating as a mechanism of defence, could also serve as a mode of communication. The infant might not only rid himself of unbearable experiences but might also create the possibility that the mother might come to understand these unconsciously. The infant could behave in such a way as "to arouse in the mother feelings of which the infant wishes to be rid" (Bion, 1967, p. 114).

In his model of the container and the contained, Bion (1962a, 1962b) outlined how, under favourable circumstances, the mother would recognize and be able to contain the infant's unmanageable experience. He talked of maternal reverie:

> This is her capacity with love to think about her infant—to pay attention, to try to understand. . . . Her thinking transforms the infant's feelings into a known and tolerated experience. If the infant is not too persecuted or too envious, he will introject and identify with a mother who is able to think, and he will introject his own now modified feelings. [O'Shaughnessy, 1988, p. 179]

According to this view, there is a continuous cycle of projection followed by introjection during which unbearable feelings are projected into the mother and returned by her to the infant in a more manageable form. Eventually, the infant not only takes in the now modified but formerly unbearable feelings, but also begins to establish an internal object capable of undertaking the functions of modifying frustration and of thinking.

What happens under favourable circumstances between infant and mother may happen in psychoanalytic psychotherapy if the therapist is able to bear the patient's projective identification, recognize it, and return it to the patient in a way that he can bear.

Countertransference

The question of the impact of the patient on the therapist has, of course, been of long-standing interest and debate. Heimann, in her classic paper "On Countertransference" (Heimann, 1950), is generally credited with opening a debate about the complexities of making use of the therapist's feelings to provide information about the patient. The central idea is that by means of projective identification the patient evokes in the therapist feelings that, if scrutinized, can contribute to the therapist's understanding. A key concern has been the extent to which feelings that belong to the therapist can be distinguished from those projected by the patient.

Recently there has been increasing interest in the way in which the therapist can be affected by the patient, not only in terms of "thoughts and feelings", but also in "propensities towards action" (Feldman, 1997, p. 227).

Betty Joseph, for example, stresses how patients make use of primitive defence mechanisms to avoid pain and conflict, and how, in therapy, they involve the therapist in their defensive armoury. She writes: "defences like projective identification, splitting, omnipotent denial are not just thought; they are in phantasy linked to the transference" (Joseph, 1983, p. 142). Joseph is here emphasizing that psychoanalytic psychotherapy is not just an intellectual activity or experience: given the primitive anxieties and defences involved, there is a pressure (often very subtle) to *act* and to induce the therapist to behave in ways that correspond with the patient's unconscious phantasy.

Such pressure may or may not be successful (in terms of getting the therapist to behave in certain ways), but even if the therapist's behaviour is not affected, his behaviour can still be given meaning that conforms to the unconscious phantasy of the patient. Such enactments or pressures to enact, if scrutinized, can provide valuable information. Tuckett comments: "enactment makes it possible to know in representable and communicable ways about deep unconscious identifications and primitive levels of functioning which could otherwise only be guessed at or discussed at the intellectual level" (Tuckett, 1995, quoted in Feldman, 1997, p. 228).

Psychic equilibrium

The Kleinian interest in primitive levels of experience in the anxieties and defences of the paranoid–schizoid position has led to a recognition that, although "our patients come to us, we and they hope to gain understanding. . . . In fact, many are against understanding" (Joseph, 1983, pp. 139–140). Patients repeat infantile defences in "the attempt to draw the analyst into behaviour that will evade painful emotional confrontations by attempting to maintain and restore an age-old system of psychic balance" (Spillius, 1988, p. 14).

Underlying this point of view is the contention that the capacity and willingness to face reality and the pain and conflict to which this gives rise is a feature of the depressive position. It is only when (either in a hypothetical general sense or at a particular moment in a session) a patient is operating firmly within the depressive position that he is capable of thought and willing to think.

Thus, although patients may present as wanting change and understanding, unless they are emotionally capable of this, they are likely to use their therapy—and, in particular, their relationship with their therapist—to avoid understanding and the psychic pain that results from it. Entering psychotherapy may, therefore, have more to do with an unconscious wish to preserve the psychic status quo, perhaps by reinforcing threatened defences, than with a wish to achieve real insight and change.

A number of Kleinian thinkers have considered how a tightly organized system of defences may be created on the border between the paranoid–schizoid and the depressive positions in a struggle to preserve a psychic equilibrium in the face of paranoid and depressive anxieties (Riviere, 1936; Sohn, 1985; Steiner, 1987, 1992, 1993).

Given the concern with such issues, it is not surprising that detailed scrutiny of the immediate present of the session has come to play a central part in the technique of many Kleinian psychoanalytic psychotherapists.

Historical reconstruction in Kleinian psychotherapy

What, then, of the historical past? What place does historical reconstruction have in Kleinian psychotherapy?

In one sense it can be argued that its place is central. To the extent that it is the patient's archaic internal world that is present in the unconscious phantasies, that are enacted in the transference, Kleinian psychotherapy can be characterized as being concerned with the reconstruction of this primitive world.

The "experiences and affective impulses . . . which he has for the time being forgotten" (Freud, 1937d, pp. 257–258) and which "he must be brought to recollect" (ibid., p. 257) are held to be the unconscious phantasies that the patient projects into the transference. The therapist carefully explicates this archaic world in the hope that the patient might be freed from its tyranny.

This, of course, begs an important question: to what extent does the unconscious phantasy of the adult reflect the internal world of the same adult in infancy or childhood? This is a complicated question. It is likely that parts of our internal world and some of our internal phantasies have a very long history indeed and may correspond to the anxieties and defences prevalent at a very early age. As we develop, however, it is axiomatic that our internal world changes, so that it is almost inconceivable that the internal world of an adult corresponds, in any overall sense, with the internal world of the same adult when a child.

The question of the historical validity of reconstruction of the internal world in psychoanalytic psychotherapy is one of considerable interest and importance. But it may be of more immediate interest to academic psychologists than to Kleinian psychotherapists. The key issue is that patients bring us their *current* anxieties, conflicts, and characteristic ways of dealing with these. They ask for our help in finding more satisfactory ways of dealing with the relationship between their inner and outer worlds. According to the Kleinian view, change and development proceed, not so much from accurate understanding of the historical past, as from the modification of underlying anxieties and defences via the understanding and interpretations of the therapist. In this sense, the historical validity of the internal world reconstructed in the psychotherapy may not be such an important issue.

But what of the patient's external past? What place do attempts to gain a clear, more accurate understanding of this have in Kleinian psychotherapy?

It may be fair to suggest that the interest in very early experience tends, paradoxically perhaps, to direct the attention of Kleinian practitioners away from the historical past. There are two key reasons for this.

1. The concern with primitive and often non-verbal communication gives rise to an interest in the acting-in in the session, in its immediate detail and the moment-by-moment changes between patient and therapist. Attention is directed not only to verbal content, but also to subtle changes in atmosphere and the ways in which non-verbal activity may provide evidence of the enactment

of primitive unconscious phantasies. Clearly, such an interest in the present tends to deflect attention away from the exploration of the historical past.

2. There is the recognition that it is only when a patient is operating (in a hypothetical general sense at a particular moment in a session) within the depressive position that he is capable of and truly willing to think. At all other points on the continuum between the paranoid–schizoid and the depressive positions, the patient is to a greater or lesser extent struggling to avoid painful reality.

Thus, patients may not wish for increased understanding as much as for the restoration or achievement of a manageable psychic equilibrium. To the extent that the patient is preoccupied with such issues, then history and its reconstruction may be used, not to genuinely promote increased understanding, but to deflect attention away from the explication of the present. Such exploration might threaten to disturb the patient's equilibrium rather than promote it.

Under such circumstances, a reaching for history may promote a false, if relatively safe, pseudo-understanding. The defensive possibilities in historical reconstruction are, therefore, of considerable concern.

But this need not always be the case, and there are times when genuine explication and understanding may be possible. It is at such times, when depressive-position functioning is to the fore, that historical reconstruction may be genuinely illuminating rather than primarily defensive.

Such illumination and understanding, if genuine, will be emotionally lively and suffused with depressive concern. It will not simply be an intellectual and defensive manoeuvre.

Historical reconstruction of this kind involves the recovery of lost objects and relationships. The attacks and distortions promulgated by the patient are diminished, and a more truthful picture of the past emerges. This process is likely to be painful; not only will the patient face the damage and distortions he has inflicted, but he will also have to face the limitations of his objects and their inability to create a perfect world. There will be mourning for a lost world, which, because it is lost, is impossible to repair. The atmosphere will be one of concern rather than of blame.

As Heimann eloquently suggests:

There are moments in the analysis when the patient recovers his lost original objects. He then dwells on memories of incidents and feelings, speaks with deep and genuine concern about them, works out what a certain episode means to him and must have meant to his mother or father, how he misunderstood them or they misunderstood him at the time, whilst he now realizes that he falsely attributed to them motives of indifference and hostility. In these thoughts and feelings there is sadness, remorse and quiet love, not paranoid hatred or self-pity. [Heimann, 1956, p. 120]

The extent to which it is possible to recover early memories in this way may, of course, be limited, and from a Kleinian point of view such historical construction may not be essential for change and development to take place. Nevertheless, a recovery of the historical past—and, perhaps more crucially, the reworking of emotional attitudes towards key figures and incidents from the past—may contribute to the development of a more benign and resilient internal world. Freed from some of the distortions and grievances from the past, the patient may evolve an internal world that is a resource that is better able to sustain him through the vicissitudes of everyday life.

Clinical example

I would like now to turn to a clinical example to illustrate some of the concepts and issues discussed above.

Mr A

This material concerns a 38-year-old solicitor, the only child of a mother with a manic-depressive illness and a rather remote father. He worked in a law centre and led a very restricted life, with no close relationships. I would like to begin with one of our early sessions.

Mr A arrived on time, took off his coat, and lay on the couch. After some silence, he said, "There's something that's bothering me, this difference between phantasy and reality". There was a silence. I wondered what he was talking about and what I could possibly say. He went on, "At the men's group last night one of the members was told by another that he was mothering him. I didn't know what they were talking about—I'm confused about what was happening—this difference between phantasy and reality."

In the subsequent silence, I was puzzled. Perhaps the patient is presenting an obvious dilemma that I just do not understand? I should surely be able to understand. Then I had a slight sense he might be putting me on the spot or intimidating me.

"It was okay last week", he said, " but I don't know any more." Another silence followed. His reference to last week reminded me that we had recently explored his difficulty at not being the therapist with me. And so I said that we had considered a similar issue here last week, about his attempting to sidestep his true position with me, which we had understood as linked with his anxiety about being a child in relation to a parent. I asked whether he might have felt clearer about these things last week, but that this was no longer so.

"Yes, but if I can think I didn't want to and wasn't trying to be a parent when I was a child, then I can be a child, which is what I want to be."

It required some thought on my part to make sense of this complicated construction, which I found quite intimidating.

Eventually, I found a way through and commented that this seemed like quite magical thinking. I had in mind here the omnipotence of his thinking, characteristic of paranoid–schizoid functioning; he thinks something and this (in phantasy) then happens. He agreed with my comment and fell into silence.

I was not convinced, in the light of our previous work and his attitude in the session, that he wanted to be a child, so I went on to say that I wondered if it really were the case that he wanted to be a child. Perhaps this was something that he found difficult and painful.

Mr A immediately responded, "Well, yes, when I let my parents take care of me they were always patronizing. I didn't like it." I said that I wondered if this might be true here. He doesn't like being a patient, although a part of him may want my help. I said I noticed that he began the session by referring to a group in which he plays a leading part. Perhaps he is telling me that he is my equal and not my patient or child. He interrupted me, "Well, yes, I feel like I'm a fraud. I don't feel like a leader." He fell silent. The tone of this comment was dead and somehow not fully convincing.

He went on to talk in a very detached way and at some length about the circumstances of his birth. Amongst other things, he talked about how his parents had only recently met when his mother became pregnant and of how he was born in a nursing home, which had recently been turned into a casino.

I found myself feeling rather confused and not really following what he was saying until he said, "I don't know if this is relevant, but my parents were thinking I was going to be a girl and hadn't thought of a boy's name when I was born". Somehow, as he made this comment, he seemed to come alive.

I had a sense that he was letting me know that something central to his view of himself could be denied by others. I said therefore that I wondered whether he also felt angry and upset when I had challenged his attempts to be my equal, as if I was almost denying his gender in a humiliating way. "Yes, it does feel the same in a way. I feel completely stuck." Silence.

I was left feeling unsure whether or not he agreed with me. His "yes" was said with little enthusiasm and qualified by "in a way". Also, it was not just he who felt stuck, but it was as if he were making me feel stuck by digging in his heels and bringing his work to a halt. He went on, "It makes me feel I must sort it out myself". I felt wounded, as if he were angrily pushing me away.

After a silence, I said that this was just the point. When I acted as a therapist, he experienced this as a terrible wounding attack on his view of himself as a potent leader. It could feel as if

I were punishing him for being a fraud. So he mustn't expose himself to this and must sort out his difficulties himself.

Although this was greeted with silence and deadness, I felt relieved. At least I'd been able to make sense of something and could not, therefore, be that stupid or useless. Although far from satisfied and not convinced I had made contact with, or helped, him (if anything, I had an uneasy sense I may have hurt him), I felt as if I had survived a kind of test.

As the therapy progressed, it became increasingly clear how difficult Mr A found it to be involved with someone who might not be useless. A close male work colleague was leaving, and this coincided with the news that the colleague had inherited a large sum of money. This emerged as the Easter break was approaching.

Mr A announced that he was applying for a rather prestigious job and was planning an exotic holiday. Eventually, I interpreted that he was attempting to give himself the comforting phantasy that he was leaving me, but this did not alter the reality that he was losing his colleague and also losing me for the Easter break.

His response was uncharacteristically reflective and moving. "I'm stunned, what I get up to, you're right . . . it doesn't make any difference, it hides the fact that he decided to leave first. I feel, well, a bit silly really."

But the reflective and accepting atmosphere soon disappeared, and the following session began with references to Mr A's envy of people who "didn't need" psychotherapy. He went on to tell me that he had felt "stupid" in the previous session. "It was like learning two times two equals four. Simple. I want to get there first." We understood how much he hated it and how small he felt when I understood something he did not. For me to make any intelligent comment felt awful to him, yet he was also aware that he needed the help and understanding that I could give him.

* * *

I think that this material demonstrates how patients make use of primitive defence mechanisms to avoid pain and conflict and that in therapy they involve the therapist in their defensive armoury. At both the level of the content of his material and at the level of what was being enacted in the transference and countertransference, the patient was preoccupied with avoiding the recognition of his dependence and the painful feelings that this evoked.

We can get a fuller picture of Mr A's defensive structure and of the unconscious phantasies that underlie it when we consider the countertransference.

Two countertransference feelings were particularly notable: (1) the feeling that I had to struggle to understand the generally dead material that Mr A brought and to bring him to life; and (2) a feeling that I was involved in a kind of contest in which I sometimes felt I had lost and at other times I had survived and won. When losing, I felt rather intimidated by the patient, and when feeling pleased with myself, I was sometimes aware of a feeling that I might have hurt him. I think this material can be understood as a drama with unconscious origins. In this unconscious phantasy, I think Mr A identified with a deadening but triumphant maternal object and used projective identification to evoke in me feelings that he could not bear himself and which he feared might overwhelm him. I was the one who was to feel and think about his feelings—for example, feeling hurt and rejected and stupid, or rather superior and triumphant. I struggled to bring these feelings alive, while he identified with his depressed and remote mother and frequently triumphed over me in my failure. On the occasions when something did make sense or came alive, it was almost as if the situation were reversed. My uneasy sense that I may have hurt him, and my vague sense of superiority may indicate that I became the triumphing, contemptuous mother, looking down on him.

Now I think there are many things that might be commented on in this clinical material. What I would like to emphasize, however, are five key features.

(1) The patient enacts an unconscious phantasy in the transference and attempts to draw me in to participate and play a part in this drama. I struggle to bring him to life, while in his identification with his depressed mother he rather contemptuously looks

down on me. At times the roles seem to reverse, and in the phantasy I become something like the remote, contemptuous mother and he the one who struggles to bring me alive.

(2) It is by paying close attention, not only to what he says (the content of his material), but also to his impact on me (the countertransference) that this becomes clear. The feeling that I was struggling to bring him alive, the sense of competition, and the associated alternation between feelings of triumph and humiliation were gradually registered and reflected upon.

As a result of this reflection on the transference as a total situation (Joseph, 1985), it was gradually possible to reconstruct the unconscious phantasy that Mr A had projected into his relationship with me. The correspondence between this unconscious phantasy and the unconscious phantasies of the patient's past is, of course, not clear. The relationship between the unconscious phantasy and the patient's objective historical experience is also unknown. At this stage, such questions are not of primary interest. Rather, the focus is on the immediate situation of the transference and countertransference, and the anxieties and defences that are being enacted in the consulting-room.

(3) I think the material illustrates how the patient can use talk about his history either defensively—to deflect attention from a problematic immediate situation—or to promote communication and increased understanding. When Mr A talked in a detached way about the circumstances of his birth, this seemed confusing, and I was unable to make use of it. It might be argued that I had simply failed to understand the significance of the content. I think, however, that if the countertransference is explored, then an alternative explanation can be given. I believe that initially, when he talked of his history in a rather dead way, the patient was trying to get away from me—possibly as a result of my previous comment. After some time, however, his anxiety abated, and he moved a little closer to depressive position functioning. This enabled him to open up communication—with the comment, "I'm stunned"—which enabled understanding to develop.

(4) Further reflection on what is happening permits the conclusion that the patient is struggling to deal with depressive anxieties and illustrates the consequent back-and-forth movement between the paranoid–schizoid and the depressive positions. Much of the

content is about the conflicts and struggles that ensue when Mr A begins to recognize his need for others, especially his therapist. This is both talked about and enacted with the therapist. For example, in the early sessions he makes use of projective identification to evoke in me unwanted feelings of insignificance and humiliation. Later, we can see the crisis provoked by the Easter break and the good fortune of his friend. He cannot bear the evidence of separateness, need, and dependency that this expresses, and he again makes use of projective identification, so that, in phantasy, I am the needy one being left and he is the one who is doing the leaving. The retreat back towards the paranoid–schizoid position is followed by a movement forward towards the depressive position, when he recognizes his need for me and allows me to help him see how difficult he finds this. Later still he moves back towards the paranoid–schizoid position as he talks about feeling "stupid" and wanting "to get there first". There is, therefore, a constant movement back and forth as the patient struggles with his depressive anxieties.

Finally, I hope it is clear that although invited to play a part in the patient's unconscious phantasy and although to some degree he may unconsciously do so, it is the therapist's capacity to reflect on the part allotted to him that is so important in promoting change. Instead of simply enacting the phantasy, if the therapist can also recognize something of what is happening, think about it, and give it back to the patient via an interpretation in a digested and manageable form, some change may be possible. Thus, I tried not to enter into competition with Mr A over which of us was the therapist but, rather, attempted to make sense of what was going on between us and gradually to try to tell him something about my observations and thoughts. Of course, however careful, sensitive, and skilled the therapist, it is likely that whatever he says— or does—will be drawn into the patient's phantasy. Indeed, it can be argued (e.g. Carpy, 1989, p. 292) that some degree of enactment is both inevitable and necessary before any thought and reflection is possible. Thus, after initially accepting my interpretations about how he was dealing with the Easter break, Mr A began to complain that my comments made him feel small, and he expressed a wish "to get there first". The phantasy of competition is re-instituted as my interpretation is incorporated into the drama. The task of the therapist is to recognize and refuse to respond to the (often very subtle) pressure to participate in such enactments, so that over time the phantasies become less pervasive, as other possibilities emerge.

A later session

I now turn to a later session that will, I hope illustrate both further movement and how, rather than serving a defensive function, historical reconstruction can promote increased understanding and development.

> Mr A came in and seemed slightly angry. After he had settled on the couch, I told him the dates of a forthcoming week's holiday break. His response seemed rather cold—he just said "yes". He went on to say, "I know this may sound rather mercenary, but will you be charging me for that week?"
>
> I said I would not be charging him and had to interrupt him to continue to say that his comment was surprising—I had not ever previously charged him for sessions during a break that I had taken.
>
> Mr A agreed with this and went on to say that on the previous day "something happened which made me wonder whether you might charge me". He went on to tell me in some detail that a parent had complained about him in a letter sent to the head of his firm. He had been involved in defending the complainant's son in a criminal case, and the son had received a custodial sentence. The letter of complaint had accused him of being cold, arrogant, and uncaring and had said that he should not be employed to defend people.
>
> Mr A talked about the lack of interest and support from his colleagues. One had offered to help him write a reply to the complaint, but none seemed emotionally available to him.
>
> I found myself feeling considerable sympathy for him, but as we had recently spent several sessions exploring how sharp and contemptuous he could be, I was also struck by the con-

tent of the complaint. I therefore acknowledged how hurt and vulnerable he felt, commented on his sense that he had not had real support, and suggested that he might feel this because of his own unease at how sharp he could be.

He half agreed with me but went on to clarify that he was not so concerned about the technical aspect of the complaint. He was more concerned about the part that concerned his behaviour when he had seen the mother and son in the Court cells after her child had been sentenced. The mother had accused the patient of being unsympathetic to her and cruel to her son. The patient was very clear that he had not behaved in this way, yet he felt exposed and vulnerable.

Mr A then went on to say that the whole incident reminded him of his relationship with his mother.

He spoke angrily about how his mother (particularly during her manic episodes) would often accuse him of not caring about her and of being cold and dismissive. This made him feel very angry, because this was just how she was towards him. When she was manic, she was cruel, and when she was depressed, she was selfish. "No wonder I've got problems and need psychotherapy", he said.

After talking about this for a few minutes, he became less angry and gradually became sad. Eventually, he said that the point was that really he wanted his mother to be with him as she was when she was "well". When she was high or depressed, it was as if she had become someone else. He cried as he went on to talk about his mother in a moving way, of her troubled childhood, of how frightened she could be before she went into mental hospital, of how ashamed she was of her illness and of her sometimes rather clumsy efforts to help him. She had hurt him, but perhaps he had hurt her too. She was not the best mother in the world, but she couldn't really help this, and it was difficult for all the family.

Referring to his response to my telling him about the break, Mr A said, "I knew you wouldn't charge me really, but, you see, when you talked about the break, I hated it. I can't stand the idea of you having a holiday with your family. It's not fair, but it's better if you're awful."

We were able to understand that when he felt hurt and excluded, a familiar drama ensued. I became a dismissive figure, not interested in him and prone to exploit him. Such a version of me protected him from his awareness of wanting me and of missing me. In this drama he became identified with a cruel and arrogant maternal object locked in battle with a hostile world. This had a long history, and he was reminded of what had happened with his mother. There had, however, been a price to pay for relief from feelings of exclusion and loss; he was left isolated in a world that was against him. His initial reaction to the news of the break was to respond in this familiar way.

The accusation of the complainant that Mr A had been arrogant and cruel, while objectively untrue, did reflect an unconscious truth and was, therefore, disturbing to him. Although he had not done the things of which he had been accused (of behaving in a dismissive and cruel way), his reaction to the complaint was to feel as if it was true (he felt uneasy, exposed and vulnerable). I think that the reason for this may have been that unconsciously he had felt on the side of the excluding authorities, looking down, perhaps with contempt, on the delinquent boy and his mother. The complaint thus served as a vehicle for the enactment of an unconscious phantasy in which objects were attacked in order to deal with loss and exclusion. In this phantasy, the patient was sometimes in the role of the "excluder" (as in Court) and sometimes in the role of the excluded (as with the break).

It now seemed as if it was possible for Mr A to begin to acknowledge and bear to know how he felt when he was left. This was true both in his relationship with his mother and in his work with me. He could also recognize what he did to protect himself from such painful feelings. The capacity to recognize what he felt, how, in the service of defence, he attacked his objects, and how his perceptions of important relationships, therefore, became distorted enabled other possibilities to emerge.

In his relationship with his mother, he could now feel concern for her and about how he had treated her. While acknowledging her difficulties and limitations, these were talked of with regret, rather than as justifying a grievance. This enabled him to recover something good and potentially strengthening in his relationship with her.

Similarly, in his view of me and of the unwelcome break, Mr A was able to tolerate his feelings of loss and exclusion and recognize his attempts to avoid these. No longer distorted by his attacks, I was available as relatively benign and helpful.

I think this session, in contrast to the earlier work, demonstrates how the patient's defensive structure has become less rigid and how he is now able to confront some of the pain he had previously been unable to contemplate. Although the nature of his difficulties and the content of his unconscious fantasies remain broadly the same as when he entered therapy, his capacity to explore these and to take in and use what I say has increased. I think this indicates a move towards the depressive position in which thinking and exploration are now a possibility.

It is also notable that in the countertransference I felt sympathy and not intimidation. I was able to think, and when I had something to say I did not experience relief or triumph but a satisfying feeling of contact. I think this provides further evidence of how the enactment between us of his unconscious fantasies of triumph and humiliation has reduced and has been replaced by an increased capacity for thought and exploration.

This movement towards depressive position functioning seems to extend to the patient's use of his history. Although initially Mr A seemed to use the reference to his mother to evade lively but painful contact and to justify a grievance ("no wonder I've got problems and need psychotherapy"), eventually he became more thoughtful and was able to acknowledge feelings of exclusion, loss, and concern.

This opened up the possibility of a relationship less infused with contempt and cruelty and involving greater love and concern. While not denying a historical reality that was far from ideal (and at times probably cruel and frustrating), the patient's link with his past now has the potential to carry a different and more hopeful meaning.

Conclusion

In this chapter I have outlined the Kleinian understanding of infant development and shown how it informs work with adult patients. I have suggested that while the Kleinian concept of position can indicate a developmental stage, it is more properly seen as a particular constellation of anxieties and defences, which, to some degree, persist throughout life. Although there is movement in normal development away from the paranoid–schizoid position towards the depressive position, this is never final and absolute. In ourselves and in our work with patients, we can observe the constant shifting between these positions. The anxiety about survival is never completely overcome, and the anxiety about separateness, dependency, and guilt is never fully worked through.

It appears something of a paradox that while Klein was a pioneer in investigating the mind of the infant, current Kleinian practice gives priority to investigating the here-and-now of the consulting-room rather than attempting to reconstruct the historical past. This apparent paradox becomes less of an issue, however, when it is appreciated that it is the contemporary manifestations of these very early states of mind, these primitive, unconscious phantasies, that are of interest to Kleinians.

I have shown how the patient's world of unconscious phantasy is explicated via detailed scrutiny of the transference and countertransference. A key feature of Kleinian psychotherapy is that, just as the mother promotes the growth and development of her infant by her capacity to understand and contain the infant's unbearable anxieties, so the therapist aims to capture and hold onto the patient's anxieties in the consulting-room. The central concern is with the immediate quality of the session. *It is the experiencing of the live interaction WITH the therapist, rather than an intellectual explanation FROM the therapist, that leads to the reconstruction of infantile anxieties and defences.* The anxieties may be experienced in a lively way, and it is therefore crucial that the therapist has the capacity to contain and digest these rather than simply to enact the object relationships with which they are associated. They can then be returned to the patient via an interpretation in a more manageable form.

Reconstruction for contemporary Kleinians is primarily, therefore, a painstaking attempt to understand the archaic world of unconscious phantasy as manifested in the present. Historical reconstruction of the patient's external world does not generally occupy centre stage.

Whether it is for a brief moment or for a more substantial period, however, when depressive-position functioning is to the fore, historical reconstruction can be genuinely illuminating and may both reflect and help to promote psychic change. For contemporary Kleinian practitioners, the central issue and concern is, therefore, not so much historical reconstruction itself, but how this is approached and the use to which it is put.

CHAPTER TWO

On the persistence of early loss and unresolved mourning

Susan Lipshitz-Phillips

In this chapter, I discuss the impact of early loss and the ways in which the personality can be constructed to keep in touch with, to commemorate, or, on the other hand, to deny such experiences, using both clinical and literary examples.

Psychoanalytic theory of psychic reality shows that reaching adulthood does not necessarily coincide with reaching maturity. Individuals remain constrained by, and live in, their past in various ways. As Freud (1920g) described it, the powerful force of the repetition compulsion refuses to allow later experiences to modify earlier, often disappointing ones. He recognized, in *Beyond the Pleasure Principle*, that the individual felt obliged to "repeat the repressed material as a contemporary experience instead of, as the physician would prefer to see, remembering it as something belonging to the past" (Freud, 1920g, p. 18). And he understood that the compulsion to repeat painful experiences was an attempt to keep them alive, perhaps to control them, and could be used psychoanalytically as a communication. When a traumatic experience breaks through the protection that the mind usually employs, the person deals with the breach in order to continue functioning, by resorting to their usual defences. This is particularly likely when they suffer loss and bereavement.

Freud (1920g) and Klein (1940) saw that repetition and denial were a rejection of memories for their patients and could therefore become the vehicle for the possibilities of psychic change. Klein (1940) developed her ideas that mourning involved dealing with anxieties and a sense of persecution as well as pining for the lost object, and furthermore she discussed a sense of triumph over the object as part of the manic defence against its loss. She said that mourning reactivated infantile patterns and was a transitory state of illness. Unless the anxieties could be metabolized and worked through, a static situation of unresolved mourning could result. Hence, adulthood has to be seen as delimited by the past, and mental life is shaped both by dominant phantasies and by environmental events.

Clinically we see this when we "read" a patient's account of his or her own history and note the re-creation of family constellations and the precision with which age-related events are reproduced. Freud's writings on love and choice of love object (1910h, 1911c, 1918b) recognize the power of the Oedipus complex in our choice of partner and the repetition from one generation to the next of unresolved unconscious feelings. Similarly, in writing about culture, Freud described how groups of people cohere on the basis of unconscious needs but can be split or get into conflict if their hostility is not held down by the group leader or a collective ethos (Freud, 1921c), such as that provided, for example, by religion.

My interest here is in how a variety of experiences of loss, ranging from the crippling early loss of a mother to the loss of place provoked by siblings' arrival can persist into adult life. I give some clinical examples and then refer to the literary description of some of these themes, as offered by Thomas Hardy in his novel, *The Well Beloved*.

Mrs E

My first patient, Mrs E, came for consultation complaining of increasingly frequent and debilitating panic attacks. She was of the same age as her mother had been when she was born, and with the break-up of her marriage Mrs E wondered whether she would ever have children. Recently she had been prevailed upon to accommodate her twin sisters; the arrival of the first coincided with the emergence of her overt symptoms, which had worsened with the arrival of the second. Mrs E was agoraphobic on the roads and felt hemmed in and severely depressed at home. She was aware that when her sisters were born she had been sent away from home, and she knew she always found them irritating. She could not, however, see any link between the past and her present sense of being crowded out until it was put to her that she was thrown back to her childhood. This seemed quickly to reduce the intensity of her symptoms. It soon emerged that as a small child Mrs E had become precociously self-sufficient in order to protect her parents from her jealousy of them as a couple and as parents to her troublesome sisters. However, her sense of losing her mother's attention preceded their birth, as her mother had been depressed in the patient's first year, pining for her father, who was often absent. As a child she had been unable to face this loss before the twins' arrival had inflicted a sudden long separation from her mother.

This old situation had been doubly revived, and the splitting she had operated by keeping her distance literally and psychically from the family was now impossible to sustain. Mrs E's resentment and hostility were in conflict with her sense of duty, and she had retreated more and more into a debilitating illness, for fear of the impact of thinking or saying what she felt. The discovery that I could bear to discuss her hatred, for example, seemed to enable her to distinguish the terrible, destructive infantile phantasies of the past and present from a real attack on the existence of her objects and to reduce her need to attack her own functioning instead. I think that the persistence of these unresolved feelings had left Mrs E vulnerable; she had only partial relationships, was often badly treated, and her underlying anxieties kept her on the move, fuelling her need to travel constantly and making her very elusive.

It is noticeable that these are quite consciously known events. Freud wrote: "Forgetting impressions, scenes or experiences nearly always reduces itself to shutting them off. When a patient talks about these 'forgotten' things he seldom fails to add, 'As a matter of fact I've always known it, only I've never thought of it'" (Freud, 1914, p. 148). So we have come to see them as neither fear nor phantasy but often-repressed reflections of an important failure in the individual's world that they were not helped to metabolize at the time, leaving therefore extensive damage. The disaster need not necessarily be a big one, but the disappointment may still feel massive. Evidently, conscious knowledge is no protection from the shock of memories returning to disturb the system, and this can be provoked by the recreation of old circumstances, as in the case of Mrs E. In her adult life they created the conditions for reworking the past or for a breakdown.

Mrs G

In this next clinical example there is an illustration of the return of a dismissed bit of family history that affected my patient's difficulties in a postpartum illness and plagued her in her struggle to mother her own child. Of the many losses suffered by her family, it seemed that the death of a child in a family boating tragedy stayed in Mrs G's mind. With the birth of her own baby, this disaster went through the protective barrier of memory and phantasy and became overwhelmingly real and part of Mrs G's intensely anxious state. She was constantly preoccupied with her baby's survival and watching over her eating and sleeping kept the patient incessantly vigilant, both day and night. It seemed that nothing could reassure her, and she was tormented by highly coloured and dramatic scenarios of disaster. At one session she reported a dream including these elements: *She was following a figure up some stairs, afraid to fall as there was no rail, and saw a tiny, thin baby left exposed at the bottom, with tribal people dancing around it in some sort of ritual. She bathed the baby, but it made a mess, so she rejected it. Then she was in an underground place like a catacomb or temple, which was flooded with water, and there was a wreck eerily visible through the half-light.*

Her associations suggested that the dream referred to the sea and the boating accident, with the wreck in the water and an awareness of a submerged temple or burial place. She saw herself inside as having a mother who allowed such an accident to occur and felt unsure she could be a good-enough mother to her own baby. In fearing that she had inherited the mantle of these neglectful parents, she tried to be beyond reproach and to outdo or even triumph over them—hence her extreme vigilance and persecutory state. In going away up the stairs and rejecting the messy baby, she was leaving it again, as if history unconsciously could only repeat itself. There is also the sense that she became omnipotent and lost any feeling of getting help from a capable aspect of the parental figures or from her therapist. At times, in the grip of this state, she was almost impossible to reach, but in the course of intensive therapy it became possible gradually to differentiate the historical from the present situations. This relieved the anxiety, and, as time went on, her daughter's survival also helped, but Mrs G continued to be vulnerable to depression and psychotic thinking.

This example raises the question of how far conscious knowledge can help in the modification of the past and therefore intervene in repetitions.

I think that there are developmental determinants in the sense that Klein (1957) discussed when in her theory of the mind she spoke of the fluctuating balance between persecutory and depressive anxieties. This is partly a given and partly reflects the ability or failure of the individual to deal with life experiences. The environment, and particularly the extent to which it offers containment, will affect how loss is borne, whether a constructive reparative process occurs, and whether a good internal object can be re-established. The mind seems to need intellectual as well as emotional knowledge for learning from experience to occur. The severity and type of loss will affect and delimit the extent of possible psychic change. Many writers—Erikson (1959), for example—assume that there is a move from activity to contemplation in the course of ageing. However, as these examples show, it is not a necessary concomitant of ageing that mature (in the sense of depressive position) functioning is achieved.

What is tolerated in our culture as adolescent exploration—for example, in having crushes and partial relationships—will be seen as a repetition if it persists unchanged into later life. Often an individual comes for therapy at the point when they realize intellectually that their behaviour is unchanged over time, but they feel powerless to alter it alone. Jaques' (1965) view on adulthood is helpful because he links maturity and having feelings of concern, guilt, and loss with recognizing the inevitability of death. This, he says, brings the mind under the dominance of the reality principle. Advancing chronological age—particularly after mid-life—makes this less easy to deny and can even lead to a greater creativity. Denial can be very persuasive, and we become attached to the familiar world of our repetitions with their enticing offer of a timeless, unchanging universe. The pain of being caught up in repetition can, on the other hand, motivate the desire to avoid it and promote change. Jaques describes adulthood as a state where "infantile depression is being worked through but with mature insight into death and destructive impulses to be taken into account" (Jaques, 1965, p. 505). He suggests that recognizing death as "real" is an important discriminator of maturity and challenges the universal unconscious belief in eternal life. What is possible for any individual depends on whether love or hate predominates in their mental life; the refusal to accept the facts of life only leads to the reinforcement of manic defences and can lead to a total retreat from psychic reality (Steiner, 1993).

This seems to help to understand the preceding examples: splitting processes severed emotional and intellectual knowledge. Through working in the transference, especially around breaks, there is an opportunity to reconstruct the links and bring them alive. As Joseph (1985) has described it, the total transference atmosphere of assumptions and inevitabilities that the patient tries to reconstitute with the therapist is a clue to the old relationships that they inhabit and part of the process of repetition. She stresses the importance of "seeing transference as a living relationship in which there is constant movement and change" and that "everything of importance in the patient's psychic organization based on

his early and habitual ways of functioning, his phantasies, impulses, defences and conflicts, will be lived out in some ways in
the transference" (Joseph, 1985, p. 454). This complex view enables
us to see why intellectual knowledge of loss or abuse, say, is no
protection against the intrusion of the damaged infantile level of
psychic functioning into later life. And unless the details of the
repetition can be traced via work in the transference and countertransference, the damage can quietly persist and perhaps become
visible to the patient only as a sudden tantrum, psychotic episode,
or destructive attack wreaking havoc in their lives. It also seems
that in some cases the splitting processes create a stasis and para-
lyse growth in a persistent way.

Jaques (1965) sees the ability to manage such destructiveness
as being linked with the capacity for creativity. Just as the extent
and type of splitting varies depending on whether the patient is
operating in a paranoid–schizoid or depressive mode, so will the
type of creativity be affected. Sometimes the unconscious invest-
ment in maintaining the status quo can be so powerful that it
paralyses life entirely, but more often it subtly structures and in-
hibits the quality of life the patient is permitted and deadens their
internal world. In the Thomas Hardy novel I refer to, there is an
example of how the hero's ability as an artist—and indeed the
subject of his sculptures—is related to his state of mind. But before
proceeding to that, I think it is important to consider what contribution environmental failure can make to these processes.

Melanie Klein (1940) described the intricacies of projective
identificatory processes operating between a mother and her infant. Depending on the "fit" between mother and infant, they form
the basis of early experience and influence how bearable primitive
anxieties are for any particular baby. The extent to which the
mother can modify her baby's anxieties will affect whether the
child is left to put together an agglomeration of partial experiences, using omnipotent phantasies, rather than creating solid internal objects. In extremis, the child is left in a private world of
communication (Bion, 1957).

Klein also allowed for the contribution made by the baby's
own endowment—especially of envy (Klein, 1957, p. 176)—in the
difficulty of modifying primitive anxieties and primitive thought.

In describing how the child's inner world is built up, Klein (1940) refers to the processes of internalization and the constant interaction in the child's experience between an "internal" and an "external" mother, one being the "double" of the other. This "double" "at once undergoes alterations in the child's mind through the process of internalization; that is to say, her image is influenced by his phantasies and by internal stimuli and internal experiences of all kinds". She goes on to say that "external situations" that follow the same route from the earliest days also "become 'doubles' of real situations and again are altered for the same reasons" (Klein, 1940, p. 346). It is therefore not difficult to extrapolate from this that particularly powerful external events can strain the defensive apparatus: the loss of the real mother, as in my next case example, means the loss of the irreplaceable object. Klein (1940, p. 353) says: "the actual loss of a loved person is, in my view, greatly increased by the mourner's unconscious phantasies of having lost his internal 'good' objects as well. He then feels that his internal 'bad' objects predominate and his inner world is in danger of disruption." She goes on to discuss how unpleasant or traumatic experiences will increase the likelihood that trust and hope will diminish and that anxieties about inner annihilation and external persecution will increase. This balance affects whether the depressive position can be established more securely or whether the paranoid–schizoid dominates. Resorting to repetition is more likely when there is less trust in "good" objects and their capacity to survive. The repetition would seem to be acting almost like a predisposition to recreate the familiar circumstances internally as well as emerging in a pattern of relationships as both memorial and communication, as discussed earlier.

The strength of resolution of these issues in treatment depends on working them through so that instead of cutting off from loss, using splitting and denial as defences, the patient is able to overcome their resistances. A "good" internal object rather than an ideal one can also now be instated. Freud (1914g, p. 155) wrote: "One must allow the patient time to become more conversant with this resistance with which he has now become acquainted, to *work through* it, to overcome it, by continuing, in defiance of it, the analytic work according to the fundamental rule of analysis."

Mr D

This final case seems to illustrate some of these themes. Mr D came for therapy in dire distress, as he tearfully explained that his family was breaking up, and he felt that nothing could be done. He wondered, however, whether I could effect a rescue. My understanding of this seemed to elicit the information that his mother had died in childbirth and he had not had a stable foster home for some time. He proceeded to describe how he had done quite well in life, formed relationships and had worked, using an independent self who was created to transcend most obstacles. He had learnt survival techniques and also looked after others, constantly reversing his early feelings of vulnerability. But lately he had become worried by his frantic panic when he felt misunderstood, and he was also finding it increasingly difficult to be away from home and family.

As the therapy progressed, it became clearer how Mr D's survival had been based on rejecting the meaning of his mother's death, although he was aware of it as a biographical fact. This he could do as long as he felt little about anyone's comings or goings: his, my own, or his family's. The illusion, fostered in his past, was maintained that none of it mattered—he could not miss what he had never known. As the worst had already happened to him, what was there to be anxious about? However, as he aged and his own son was leaving home, Mr D was faced again with his undigested, unmourned loss. His sense of a gap, of something missing, was revived, and his solution of being parented himself while parenting his son was no longer viable as a container for the projection of his own neediness. It also gradually emerged how Mr D had used a secret relationship to his dead mother—unconsciously the ideal, perfect object—to help him to face disappointments in life. She had apparently kept him going, but also kept him separated from his real, available objects and what they offered him. This left him lonely.

Jaques (1965) points out that if death has no meaning, then neither does life, so that any creative efforts the individual makes are felt as alien and external. So Mr D found that his external creation of a new father/mother/son family was not sufficient to blot out his own past. Unless he could mourn the loss of his manic defensive solution, he would be unable to develop. Recognizing that the therapy, rather like the foster care, was not the same thing as growing up in his own family seemed to be vital. It meant that I was neither omnipotent nor confused about these differences, and it finally allowed space for his mother's existence and her loss to be faced and mourned. His survival in the future would now be seen against this background and that of his own ageing and death. The way Mr D had arrived in treatment seemed to be comprehensible, after some years of therapy, as carrying these old problems with him; he needed attention to the earliest traumatic and confused situation of his life in order to develop.

Thomas Hardy's *The Well Beloved*

Thomas Hardy's 1897 novel, *The Well Beloved*, offers a powerful literary example of the themes I have been discussing. Although Hardy wrote two alternative endings to his novel, the resolution they offer is the same. *The Well Beloved* can lay claim to exploring the same terrain as Proust's *A la Recherche du Temps Perdu*. Both recognize the importance of memories and the way repetition of personal history affects the possibilities of loving and creativity.

Hardy's story is a phantasy, with little pretence at realism or credibility. It follows the story of Jocelyn Pierston's life and his fascination with three generations of women from one family. Jocelyn, a sculptor, was born on the rocky Isle of Slingers whose quarries supplied stone for buildings in London and for his own works of art. He had not known his mother, who died early in his life, and his relation to his father is distant. The story begins with his return from travels abroad to see his father. He knew from boyhood—Hardy tells the reader—that he was subject to transient involvement with a "love" that located itself in one woman after another, migrating endlessly. This time it took up its abode in the body of his neighbour and distant kin, Avice Caro, whom he met on his return to the island. Under this spell, he quickly asked her to marry him, but when she refused to consummate their love before marriage, as required by ancient custom, he lost interest.

On his journey back to London he met Marcia Bencomb and fell in love with her, but she soon left him.

In his loss, Jocelyn was able to work successfully at his sculpture, dedicated himself to the study of female beauty, and was rewarded by becoming a Royal Academician. However, he was constantly plagued by his well-beloved:

> Essentially she was perhaps of no tangible substance a spirit, a dream, a frenzy, a conception, an aroma, an epitomized sex, a light of the eye, a parting of the lips. God only knew what she really was; Jocelyn Pierston did not. She was indescribable. Never much considering that she was a subjective phenomenon vivified by the weird influences of his descent and birthplace, the discovery of her ghostliness, of her independence of physical laws and failings had occasionally given him a sense of fear. He never knew where she would be, whither she would lead him. [Hardy, 1897, p. 34]

He discovered that his plaster-and-stone images of his phantasies tapped into public taste and brought him popular acclaim.

His friend, Summers, observed that one day he would meet his match in a woman whose own well-beloved would flit about like Jocelyn's. He advised Jocelyn not to marry and warned him that as he grew older, the situation would become untenable. This is of interest to us, for here there seems to be a presentiment that with increasing age this problem of love would have to be faced in new ways.

Twenty years passed, and now aged 40, Jocelyn returned to the island, where he learned of Avice's death. Filled with memories of her, he was astonished to see her double, young and unchanged, incarnated in a local girl. He learnt that this girl was no vision, but Avice's daughter, and he pursued her. He moved back to the island, but found that she was afraid of his attentions, and she finally confessed that she, too, had trouble with a migrating image of her beloved. It roved from man to man as his did from woman to woman. Undaunted, Jocelyn decided to try at least to look after her, and took her back to London with him. Later he discovered that she was secretly already married and was pregnant, so he brought about reconciliation between this Avice the second and her husband Isaac.

For twenty more years Jocelyn worked and travelled and knew nothing further of the couple's life, until by chance he heard that Marcia had gone back to the island. Simultaneously, he received a letter from Avice the second, saying that she was now widowed and would like to see him. Now aged 60, Jocelyn again returned to the island to find her child, now 20, the latest incarnation of his original love, Avice. Jocelyn felt driven to court this third Avice, although the disparity in their ages was shocking to both. Their marriage was encouraged by the girl's mother—Avice the second. The young girl was discovered in time to have a lover of her own age, who was in fact Marcia's stepson, and these two eloped. Avice the second then died, and after all these shocking events Jocelyn fell ill. He recovered to find that Marcia had nursed him back to life. In the twilight of the sick-room, Jocelyn saw her as miraculously young and unchanged. She told him that this was an illusion of makeup and bravely offered to reveal herself to him without artifice.

> The cruel morning rays—as with Jocelyn under Avice's scrutiny—showed in their full bareness, unenriched by addition, undisguised by the arts of colour and shade, the thin remains of what had once been Marcia's majestic bloom. She stood the image and subscription of Age—an old woman, pale and shrivelled, her forehead ploughed, her cheek hollow, her hair as white as snow. [Hardy, 1897, p. 201]

In seeing her so, Jocelyn was relieved to acknowledge his own ageing, so long denied; gratefully and without regret he saw the departure of his plaguing phantasies. With them went his interest in art and in beauty, and he gave up his studio, feeling that a curse had been removed from his life. He and Marcia, to the delight of the islanders, settled into a close relationship. They reconciled Avice the third with her husband, and Jocelyn devoted himself to good works on the island. The endless romantic cycle was broken by their acceptance of the reality of time, age, and death. The curse of Aphrodite was broken, and Jocelyn found true love when he joined in the reality of being human and therefore subject to the laws of time.

* * *

Werman and Jacobs (1983) discussed *The Well Beloved* as an example of infatuation, "a painful, repetitive and finally absurd ritual"
(p. 448) that Jocelyn is compelled to enact until the end of his life.
They list the characteristics of infatuation in the story; the lover
having an intense, irrational, dreamlike experience of an idealized
object. They point to the fundamental ambivalence and how, as
flaws in the beloved inevitably become visible through closer acquaintance, so disappointment follows. Werman and Jacobs (1983)
go on to give biographical details to link Hardy's personal experience with his fiction. For example, they wonder how he could
have written such a story if it were not for his own difficult experience of marriage, his youthful closeness to a much older woman,
and his several love affairs.

While it might be interesting to pursue this line and wonder
about the function Hardy's fiction served for its author in healing
his past and present, I want instead to briefly discuss this notion
of infatuation, so vividly described in *The Well Beloved*. Werman
and Jacobs (1983) refer to Kernberg (1974) as saying that "people
who become infatuated are incapable of establishing object relation; infatuation is a repetition compulsion whose origins are in
developmental failures" (p. 448). Certainly Hardy's hero, Jocelyn
Pierston, seems unable to process loss or face depressive anxieties
until the last phase of his life. The mother earth of the island and
the perfect feminine principle embodied in *The Well Beloved* were
entwined and seem to represent a powerful maternal imago.
Given that Jocelyn did not know his mother, there is a feeling that
he is intensely searching for some real embodiment of her in order
to evade his loss. Unconsciously, his lost mother is the model of an
ideal woman, and his difficulty in seeing her as a whole is epito-
mized by the description of the partial features (voice, aroma, and
lips) that captivate him in turn. This seems to depict the operation
of the infantile mind, experiencing only fragmented aspects of the
mother at first, as described by Klein. Without a real person who
might become coherent through reality-testing, Jocelyn is left with
a series of part objects that momentarily appear to cohere and
create a passing facsimile of perfection. His experience is like "fall-
ing in love", but he is constantly faced with the absence of a real
model for his affections as the fascination wears off. His experi-

ences with three generations of Avice Caro dramatize this inability to get away from his early loss and his imprisonment in the repetition compulsion.

Hardy remarks that Jocelyn Pierston does not produce great art. This seems to represent awareness that sublimation is only partially successful as a solution to his psychic difficulties, as well as preventing him from really loving. Once Jocelyn accepts the reality of ageing, he loses interest in his art, as if its source were pathological. He also turns to repairing the island that his father's quarrying has ruined, as if to repair the mother earth. His first concern is said to be to restore clean drinking water to the local people—surely a significant symbolic gesture of reparation.

* * *

In the case material and in the portrayal of the struggles of Jocelyn in Hardy's novel, the overshadowing presence of early loss is visible. The persistent effects of catastrophic loss, particularly in delaying the recovery of what Klein (1940, p. 362) thought of as harmony in the inner world, is evident as the world is stripped of its goodness, leaving the infantile mind in the grip of terror that it will not be able to survive. At such times it seems that all friendly figures have deserted him. In the relatively ordinary developmental experiences of the series of losses proceeding from the first absence of the breast, the child builds up stamina and has the memory of surviving to draw on. When there has been an unacceptable loss, there is a really lost, damaged object inside, reinforcing the belief in fragility and a reminder that survival is not guaranteed.

In conclusion, I return to Klein's (1940, p. 344) paper on mourning, where she says, "In my view there is a close connection between the testing of reality in normal mourning and early processes of the mind. My contention is that the child goes through states of mind comparable to the mourning of the adult, or rather that this early mourning is revived whenever grief is experienced in later life. The most important of the methods by which the child overcomes his states of mourning is, in my view, the testing of reality." The clinical material and fictional account outlined here reflect some of the different defensive arrangements that can be made to defer or refuse to face the reality of loss. The reactivation of old grief in later life can be the undoing of these old, apparently acceptable compromises between knowledge and feeling and show up the costs of maintaining these structures.

The first patient, Mrs E, developed a somatic solution, and her experiences of panic led her to worry that she was going to black out, lose consciousness, or die. She had medical investigations to reassure herself that she was not physically ill, only to find that she had cleared the way for worrying about her mental state. It seemed almost preferable to lose her mind or to have to go to bed and retreat from the world than to face exploring the contents of her mind—especially the hatred of her siblings and the sense of loss of her mother's attention.

Mrs G, on the other hand, suffered from alternating manic and depressive states. She often retreated into a world in which she omnipotently controlled things and expelled badness into the outside world. Unfortunately, it returned to plague her in the form of persecuting anxiety that her baby would not survive, and she felt that she had to watch over the badness to try to keep her safe. Hence her identification with a bad mother inside operated to spoil any good qualities either she or her objects had. She felt that the only safe place for the baby had been inside her, and ever since their separation at birth she felt that the world was untrustworthy. The additional fact that members of the family had died young seemed to be further evidence of the dangers; thus the cycle of mistrust persisted.

In Mr D's case, an apparently much more functional solution had been possible as he had created a new family to provide him with what had been missing in his own infancy, and this external reparation seemed to help him survive quite well. However, predicated as it was on the denial of the fact of his mother's death, it was fragile, and his infantile rage, loss, and distress kept reappearing to remind him of it.

Perhaps one could characterize Jocelyn Pierston's solution, in Hardy's story, as one of obsessional repetition; while he did not retreat from life and unbearable reality into psychosis, he certainly is described as maintaining massive denial of natural processes.

The consequences were that he could not form a partnership nor have a family, nor could he enjoy his work. He suffered from the pursuit by his well-beloved phantom until he could finally face the fact that all three of the Caro women were lost to him. This was the beginning of his recovery.

The child wants to grow up and have all the perceived advantages of maturity and power. However, as I hope I have illustrated, this appears on closer acquaintance to be a complex and erratic progress, since the unconscious forces of repetition are ranged against us. As psychotherapists trying to think about and intervene in such processes, we do well to be vigilant to their appearance in the transference.

CHAPTER THREE

Interrelationships between internal and external factors in early development: current Kleinian thinking and implications for technique

Jessica Sacret

I n this chapter I want to explore, in a necessarily somewhat schematic way, some of the issues implicit in current theoretical developments in the Kleinian literature and to elaborate some of their implications. More specifically, I want to focus on the relationship between internal and external influences in psychic development, insofar as these are highlighted in the discussion of issues underlying the understanding and treatment of patients whose therapy seems to present particular difficulties by virtue of the predominance in the personality of what has come to be known widely in the literature as a "pathological organization" of the personality (Spillius, 1988). For example, Joseph (1975) has described "patients who are difficult to reach"; Steiner (1993) uses the notion of the "psychic retreat"; and Rosenfeld (1971) has elaborated the concept of "destructive narcissism". Others in the Kleinian tradition have also written on the subject of this now well-documented albeit diverse phenomenon.

The notion of the "pathological organization" is of a complex system of defences "characterized by extremely unyielding defences and which function to help the patient to avoid anxiety by avoiding contact [I would say, intimate contact] with other people and with reality" (Steiner, 1993, p. 2). The idea also encompasses widely differing phenomena encountered in the consulting-room: withdrawal, stuckness, or deadness on the one hand, or destructive and self-destructive behaviour on the other. Joseph (1989b) describes the ways in which patients can appear to be making progress, but this is never maintained. Thinking about patients who could be described in such terms, and in perusing the literature, I found it helpful to disentangle my thoughts about seminal Kleinian concepts such as "the death instinct", "envy", and "destructiveness", and how these notions link with the aetiology of the pathology in question.

In my clinical work I have found that many—although not all—of the patients who seemed to have the most difficulty in allowing change, or who seemed to be unable or unwilling to make use of the therapy, were also those patients who presented histories of traumatic experiences, whether sexual, physical, or emotional, including traumatic neglect or loss. This made me think carefully about the relative influences of intra- and extra-psychic forces and their interplay in the difficulties displayed by my patients. It also made me consider more fully the implications for technique of understanding the pathological organization in terms of its aspect as defensive against trauma originating from the environment.

The emphasis of Kleinian thought has developed from its early, perhaps somewhat exclusive focus on the intra-psychic world of phantasy, where phantasy is thought to be the primary factor in psychic development, to a more fully interpersonal view, via Bion's work (1962a, 1962b) on containment, which gave a crucial role to the mother's capacity for reverie. Recently, we have seen the publication of a volume of papers from writers influenced by Klein on the issue of trauma—that is, the impact of external, albeit extreme, events on the psyche (Garland, 1998). In that volume, Bell points out that the relationship between the internal world and external events is often discussed as if they were opposing categories. However, from a psychoanalytic point of view, he says, we are interested in "how, in the interplay of projection and introjection, external experiences are represented, internalised and dealt with" (Bell, 1998, p. 168). In reading the early Kleinian literature, one can gain the impression that the role of external factors in development is negligible or non-existent; that pathology is always and exclusively the result of innate destructiveness, linked with the death instinct; and that the related concept of constitutional envy is entirely responsible for the existence of a weak ego linked with the inability to internalize the good breast.

Although this characterization is presumably somewhat of a caricature of what Kleinians actually believed, this is often the impression given and the view held of Kleinians by other psychoanalytic schools. As Spillius points out, "Both Klein and her followers have often been accused of overemphasizing the negative" (Spillius, 1988, p. 7). It seems that when Klein first formulated her theories, the part played by aggression and innate destructiveness, which she linked to the death instinct, was emphasized both by herself and by other analysts just because she gave more weight to them as factors in the formation of pathology than did Freud (see Hinshelwood, 1989, who gives the history). A consequence of this, allied to her equally controversial view that unconscious phantasy is present from birth (Klein, 1958), meant that the early Kleinian literature seemed to reflect a view that the aggressive and destructive phantasy of the child was not only dominant but overwhelmingly pre-eminent in the causation of its pathology. Any potential influence of the environment, in the shape of maternal and familial failure, was not emphasized.

An eminent example of this is Segal's (1964) seminal work, *Introduction to the Work of Melanie Klein*, where the discussion is carried on almost exclusively in terms of the child's phantasies, projections, and introjections, and no mention is made of any reciprocal impact the maternal figure might have on the child's defences and psychic development. However, since Bion (1962a, 1962b) has made the basis of psychic health the relationship between container and contained, a focus has developed whereby maternal and environmental failure are sometimes offered as relevant to the understanding of pathology. In the body of current Kleinian thinking, thus, there has been a movement towards a greater recognition and acknowledgement of the contribution played by the mother and the parental couple, an inevitable movement following the general acceptance of the theory of containment, which is discussed below.

Klein became aware, by the 1950s, of the sorts of criticisms outlined above, that she ignored influences of external reality, and she was at pains to spell out her position. Envy, she wrote, is to some extent constitutional, though varying individually in strength and interacting from the beginning with external circumstances.

> Furthermore, whether or not the child is adequately fed and mothered, whether the mother fully enjoys the care of the child or is anxious and has psychological difficulties over feeding—all these factors influence the infant's capacity to accept milk with enjoyment and to internalise the good breast. [Klein, 1957, p. 179]

Spillius emphasizes the point, and to my mind makes the characterization of envy truly object-relational. She writes that:

> The expression of envy, and indeed of love and hate in general, occur and develop in relationships with objects, so that one can never meet the constitutional component unmodified by experience. Nor can one tell, from the perspective of the consulting-room, how much of a patient's envy is constitutional, how much has developed because of his experiences with objects, or how much is the result of the process of interaction between the two. What one can tell from the way he behaves in the consulting-room is what his envy is like in his internal world now, how severe it is, how it expresses itself in reaction to his analyst, and what defences he uses. [Spillius, 1993, p. 1201]

Spillius is acknowledging that it is impossible to prove or disprove the existence of the death instinct. Clinicians working in the Kleinian tradition do not find it difficult to believe that something intrinsically destructive might be at work, linked with the operation of the death instinct, whilst the non-Kleinian may see it in more purely defensive terms. Experienced clinicians working in the field disagree on the issue. (For example, see Rosenfeld, 1971a, on destructive narcissism, in reply to Kernberg's, 1967, attempt at a rebuttal.)

However, as Steiner suggests, "It is not necessary to resolve controversial issues about the death instinct to recognise that there is often something very deadly and self-destructive in the individual's make-up which threatens his integrity unless it is adequately contained" (Steiner, 1993, p. 4).

He thus acknowledges that we do not have to believe in the death instinct to recognize destructiveness and envy in a patient. To my mind, what is important is how we think of the interplay between internal and external influences in the operation of what appears to be destructive or self-destructive behaviour.

Klein always placed more importance on the death instinct than did Freud, because her work with small children revealed the extent of their aggressive phantasies and consequent fear of retaliation. She believed that the powerfully harsh superego she encountered must be an early manifestation of the death instinct, of which, like Freud, she said that a portion is directed outwards and becomes, for her, linked with the notion of envy, whilst the portion remaining within becomes directed towards the ego. This internally directed death instinct, in post-Kleinian conceptualization, becomes the basis for destructiveness and self-destructiveness and for the formation of the pathological organization. Thus in Klein's view, we are born with disintegrative tendencies due to the operation of the death instinct with its characteristic mode of operation of attacks on linking.

Segal (1993) gives a helpful clarification of the psychological impact of the life and death instincts. She points out that pain and anxiety come from the urge to live; pain and conflict are an inevitable aspect in living. Death, on the other hand, is the absence of conflict and is the desire for oblivion. The experience of need, the drive that connects us to others, can be dealt with in two alternative ways. The life-oriented way manifests itself in the drive to satisfy needs, which leads to object-seeking and love. The death-instinct-driven way is to annihilate the need, or the perception of need, or to attack the ego that perceives the need.

Early writings on sabotaging phenomena emphasize the dominance of "bad" over "good" parts of the self (Meltzer, 1973; Rosenfeld, 1971a). Others focus on the operation of the destructive superego (Brenman, 1985; O'Shaughnessy, 1997). Sohn (1985) and

Rey (1979, 1994) have also written in this area; and Joseph (1989b) has made a unique contribution. A developing line of thought has been to think in terms of a fixed constellation of defences, accounting for the power and persistence of the resistance to change. This notion was elucidated by O'Shaughnessy (1981), who described a psychic system conceived of as a defensive organization operating in a systematic way, as opposed to the previous general idea of defences acting in a comparatively piecemeal way. A paper by Segal (1972) describes a delusional system developed as a defence against annihilation. A crucial aspect of such a structure is that it is organized around omnipotent phantasies and defences.

Spillius summarizes the current Kleinian thinking:

> There are two main strands of thought in the idea of the pathological organization. The first is the dominance of the bad self over the rest of the personality; many authors point out a perverse, addictive element in this bondage, indicating that it involves sado-masochism, not just aggressiveness. The second strand is the idea of development of a structured pattern of impulses, anxieties and defences that root the personality somewhere in between the paranoid–schizoid and depressive positions. This pattern allows the individual to maintain a balance, precarious but strongly defended, in which he is defended against the chaos of the paranoid–schizoid position, that is, he does not become frankly psychotic, and yet he does not progress to a point where he can confront and try to work through the problems of the depressive position with their intrinsic pain. There may be shifting around, and at times an appearance of growth, but an organization of this kind is really profoundly resistant to change.... There is considerable variation in the psychopathology of pathological organizations, but the analyses of these individuals tend to get stuck, either to be very long, only partially successful, or sometimes interminable. [Spillius, 1988, pp. 195–196]

Whilst Joseph (1982) expresses a common view in her belief that the pathological organization is both a defence against, and the expression of, the death instinct and leaves it at that, Rosenfeld (1978, 1986) cites deprivation by the external object, both in the past and the present, as a factor.

Steiner has particularly elaborated the notion of the pathological organization, which he prefers to call a "psychic retreat". He suggests that such an organization "serves to bind, to neutralize and to control primitive destructiveness whatever its source, and is a universal feature of the defensive make-up of all individuals" (Steiner, 1993, p. 4). I note here that Steiner is careful to state that although he thinks primitive destructiveness is universal, he refers to it as defensive and is wanting to make it clear that he is not assuming the existence of innate destructiveness implying a belief in the death instinct. He also cites trauma and neglect as causative in the formation of the pathological organization.

I have accentuated the developing tendency for failures in parenting function to be mentioned in descriptions of pathology, because it appears to me that the view we hold on this issue has important implications for technique. Bion says that

. . . on some occasions the destructive attacks on the link between patient and environment, or between different aspects of the patient's personality have their origin in the patient, in others, in the mother. [Bion, 1959, p. 106]

Britton, too, puts it that, "on the one hand there was the patient's inborn disposition to excessive destructiveness, hatred and envy; on the other there [is] the environment which denies to the patient the use of the mechanisms of splitting and projective identification" (Britton, 1992a, p. 109–110).

Bion's notion of containment involves the mother's capacity to accept and modify, through reverie, the baby's projections of terror, rage, and envy, and of proto-mental and beta elements that are unmanageable to the infant's psyche. An inability to accept and contain projections on the part of the mother can result in an experience of nameless dread for the infant and a sense that his communications are stripped of meaning. Hence, although there may be an innate disposition towards destructiveness, a crucial factor in the infant's development is the mother's capacity to contain and modify that destructiveness. In the view of Hyatt Williams (1998, and personal communication), the death instinct has to be modified by the containing mother if severe pathology is to be avoided. Britton suggests that a vital contribution to the ıother's containing function is the father's capacity to contain the mother in her relationship with the baby.

According to Britton, Bion suggested that "if this relationship between mother and infant goes badly wrong, instead of a helpful superego, an 'ego-destructive superego' develops . . . when containment goes wrong in some people, it produces a part of themselves opposed to themselves . . ." (Britton, 1992a, p. 107).

This would be the state of affairs that leads to the development of the ego-destructive superego, and the elaboration of this structure in terms of internal objects that attack the ego can result in a pathological formation. In the same paper, Britton goes on to make the interesting point that he has noticed that patients whose problems stem from parental difficulties in containment are often very responsive to analytic work, in distinction from patients whose more severe pathology, he believes, implies an innate component.

A very problematic consequence of inadequate containment is when any change is felt by a patient to be a step on an inevitable descent into chaos and the terrors of fragmentation. There has to be some sense of psychic continuity for there to be the possibility of change. Otherwise it will be experienced as "catastrophic" (Bion, 1967). The underlying anxiety of someone in an uncontained state of mind is described in graphic terms by Britton as resulting in the phantasy of incarceration or disintegration, the only alternatives being a deathly container or exposure in a shattered world, as Rey (1979) describes it. Britton points out that the movement between the paranoid–schizoid and depressive positions is not just an oscillation backwards and forwards between the two, but represents the process of learning and change throughout life; that we are always having to deal, if we can, with the terror of letting go of certainties in order to allow the possibilities of change, new thinking, and the potentiality of new situations to occur, a process that can go on indefinitely.

Although the term "trauma" is in general use throughout the non-Kleinian literature, Baranger, Baranger, and Mom (1988) point out that Klein uses the term "trauma" hardly at all. Hinshelwood (1989), in his *Dictionary of Kleinian Thought*, omits it completely. Baranger et al. suggest that in Klein, the concept of trauma is absorbed into the general anxiety situation of the paranoid–schizoid position and that it "shifted somewhat . . . towards the term 'anxiety situation'... which only partly covers the Freudian concept of the traumatic situation" (Baranger et al., 1988, p. 121).

However, this way of thinking has changed, as indicated by the publication of the book *Understanding Trauma* (Garland, 1998), which contains many papers by analysts of the Kleinian tradition. Bell, in his discussion of "External Injury and the Internal World" describes the traumatic situation as "the breaking through (often described as a breakdown) of unmanageable anxiety and mental pain; a breakthrough which is brought about by a combination of internal and external factors" (Bell, 1998, p. 167). Some major life events, loss, profound life changes, or catastrophic events like the sinking of a boat or a train crash are obvious sources of trauma. In the present period of sensitivity to issues surrounding sexual abuse, we are also only too painfully aware of these phenomena and their psychic consequences, often termed "traumatic stress disorder".

As I have suggested above, Kleinian writers, until recent decades, have perhaps been wary of acknowledging the contribution of environmental failures, at least in their writings, in contexts less obvious than that of sexual abuse or gross violence or neglect. The analytic method is to examine the part played by patients in their own pathology—in particular, the role of unconscious phantasy. However, to acknowledge the part played by extra-psychic failure in no way denies the importance of phantasy. Because Kleinians have—rightly, in my view—insisted on the importance and universality of unconscious phantasy (Isaacs, 1948) as underlying all thought processes and all behaviour, this does not mean that there is not a clinical responsibility to tease out, with every patient, insofar as it is possible, any contribution from the extra-psychic environment. Steiner states that

> pathological organizations have a particular role to play in the universal problem of dealing with primitive destructiveness. This affects the individual in profound ways, *whether it arises from external or internal sources*. ... Traumatic experiences with violence and neglect in the environment leads to the internalisation of violent disturbed objects which *at the same time serve as suitable receptacles for the projection of the individual's own destructiveness*. [Steiner, 1993, p. 4, italics added]

Thus it is by no means a question of evading responsibility for destructiveness, rage, or envy, but of disentangling the projections into internal objects whilst acknowledging to the patient the parental failure when it exists in reality, insofar as this can be ascertained.

In many clinical situations there may be traumas that cannot be known about but only inferred through the countertransference, as in the trauma of non-containment. Or there may be other infantile traumas because of other parenting failures that are not obvious in the clinical situation and may only show themselves through the medium of apparently destructive behaviour. There is the possibility, which can be hard to detect, of parental projection into the infant, a phenomenon that can be traumatic if it is in the form of a violent evacuation. Bell (1998) makes the point that an external event, which may appear altogether trivial, can have a traumatizing effect on an individual because of the particular meaning it has for him. We need as clinicians to be aware of these possibilities of traumatic occurrence that the patients themselves may not be aware of. To attribute responsibility to a patient in connection with a traumatizing incident is to risk re-traumatizing them and may certainly lead to hostile and destructive responses.

An experience of trauma, which may be linked with catastrophic fears of terrifying fragmentation, may be defended against, I have argued, by means of a pathological organization or psychic retreat. I have shown that it is well agreed that inadequate containment can itself be traumatic. When a patient is close to a traumatic trigger, that may be the time when he or she is the most destructive. It is therefore important to understand what may be at stake for the patient when as therapist one may be under tremendous pressure from countertransference reactions to enact a critical, angry, or sadistic response.

In the context of the most horrific abuse one can imagine, Johns, in his review of *Treating Survivors of Satanist Abuse* (Sinason, 1994), makes the point that the book "raises considerations about the role of trauma in the genesis of mental illness and how the developmentally appropriate defences that are available to the immature child are used in an effort to protect it from the overwhelming impact of the trauma but will then result in maturational distortions ... there are important matters concerning technique because the treatment of such brutalized victims has the possibility of retraumatization, either because of disbelief, or by a refusal to value some conception of the patient's personal history that would allow reconstruction of the horrific past from within the transference and countertransference experiences" [Johns, 1998, p. 1257]

I have argued that the same holds true when dealing with less obvious and less brutal abuse than that which Johns is describing, but which is nonetheless truly traumatic for the individual. In an earlier paper (Sacret, 1998), I have argued for the necessity of holding on to the healthy and sane part of the patient when under siege from the attacks, overt or covert, from a patient who is at that moment trying to keep the therapy from touching aspects of themselves that are felt to be unbearable and catastrophic. I would like to restate some theoretical and technical points about omnipotent defences when working with patients in these states, usually described as borderline.

When there has been a failure in the global situation of early containment, or other early trauma, primitive omnipotent defences are maintained when in normally healthy development, they are largely given up under the developing influence of the sense of reality, what Freud (1911b) referred to as the "reality principle", to be revived at times of particular stress, or as the result of trauma later in life (Garland, 1998). At the same time, there is the part of the personality, linked with the pleasure principle, that wishes to hold on to phantasies of omnipotence whether or not there has been any failure. Early omnipotence with its phantasy of possession of the mother/breast is thus a normal state of the primitive mind, related to the early dominance of the pleasure principle (Freud, 1911b).

The early response to frustration, the hallucinatory omnipotent phantasy of the need-fulfilling breast, has to be replaced by the recognition of a need that is not being met and the possibility of containing the frustration. If things go wrong, the early and normal phantasy of possession of the breast can become a denial of dependency and vulnerability consequent on the phantasy of omnipotent control, associated with its characteristic hallmarks, grandiosity and manic defences. There are massive projections into the mother, and later into other important figures, if containment is inadequate, as a way of getting rid of unwanted feelings and to deny separation.

If containment and early care is good enough, thinking evolves in the gap between the experience of the need and its satisfaction and aids the process of tolerating frustration. If it is not, omnipotent phantasies persist in the form of the phantasied discharge or evacuation of unwanted, unmanageable sensations and feelings into the object. This has the dual function of ridding the psyche of unbearable feelings of rage, terror, and pain and of denying separation, as the object is now felt to contain large aspects of the self. The result is also a state of confusion of which the severity varies with the extent of the projections.

When, as a result of progress in therapy, omnipotent defences are threatened, a normal response is rage (Rosenfeld, 1971b). How this rage is understood and interpreted is crucial in the negotiation of this stage of the therapy. It seems to me that there can be two different aspects to this rage, distinguishable in principle but not necessarily in the clinical situation, which need recognition in the interpretations made. One component I would link with libidinal aspects of the personality, which relates to real failures in parenting and which I therefore think of as "realistic" rage. I think of this as "libidinal" because it seems to me to express a healthy wish for good-enough containment and parenting. This rage is directed at early failures that may have left a legacy such as, for example, an unalterable tendency to experience any meaningful loss as traumatic and/or a persistent potentiality to experience terror, pain, dread, or terrifying states of fragmentation and disintegration. It seems to me that this anger deserves recognition and the failure acknowledgement before a patient can move on to accept the pain of the reality. In the transference this becomes directed at the therapist as the present-day representative of parental failure, and one can see very clearly why Freud spoke about the transference as a defence against the recognition of reality. The rage can be used also to function as a defence against the pain of reality, which contains the normal but inevitable pains of loss and separation that expose the patient to envy and jealousy.

On the other hand, there can be a rage that appears more deadly and destructive or self-destructive. This kind of rage stems from an omnipotence that hates reality, hates the conflict between love and hate, and hates the inevitable pains of living. This part of the personality demands control, certainty, and invulnerability. It operates like a dictator. It attacks the healthy part for being needy and dependent and hates the therapist for arousing those feelings. This kind of rage I think of as emerging from the "psychotic" part of the personality. It tends to be uncontained and uncontainable. Although it may also be, theoretically, understood as being defensive, at least in part, in being linked with profound failures in containment or massive early trauma, it becomes invested with a quality more connected to the death instinct. There can be pathological splitting with fragmentation and violent expulsion into objects, including the therapist (Bion, 1957). It is at this point that the therapist needs all his or her own capacity to contain their own countertransference because the patient may be intending to elicit in the therapist an angry, condemning, or sadistic response. The patient can then triumph in the therapist's "vulnerability" and in their status of victim. Vulnerability and dependency may be projected into the therapist, who is then derided for not being omnipotent.

The more containing and realistic the therapist is, the more the psychotic part of the patient may intensify its modus operandi. It is crucial at this point for the therapist to keep in mind the non-psychotic part that wants to be able to depend on help and to progress, and to try to talk to that part of the patient's personality, even when this healthy part seems to be entirely absent or completely submerged by the psychotic part (Bion, 1957). The therapist may be attacked for being the representative of sanity or reality, although this will be dressed up as something that sounds more like a realistic grievance. The omnipotent part of the patient may masquerade as healthy and be full of subtle strategies for representing the omnipotent position as the normal and sane one, off-loading responsibility for destructive behaviour onto the therapist (Lucas, 1992).

With some or all of these differing aspects of anger, rage, and destructive and self-destructive behaviour operating in a clinical situation, it can be an impossible task to do justice to them all. However, I believe that the important point is that a person who is in the grip of a defensive system like a pathological organization may have suffered early traumatic circumstances that require sympathetic hearing (Rosenfeld, 1986), even though the "realistic" rage may be associated or fused with a more psychotic rage, which has to be stood up to with firmness (Lucas, 1992). This is where the work becomes very difficult, as the defences are powerful, as has been described. The perverse strategies that may emerge at this point may also be very hard to bear for the therapist, and it is helpful to keep in mind the terrors that may be being defended against. Such a patient will find it hard to accept and work through the reality of separation and the necessity of giving up phantasies of omnipotence. He or she may also find it extremely painful to acknowledge the need for reparation to parental figures, internal or external, who are also human and who may equally have been inadequately contained or traumatized themselves. This pain, depressive and reparative, is very hard to work through for such a patient. Rage, especially when it has a psychotic component, can also be expressed for prolonged periods in destructive or perverse ways and used as a defence against the pain and the acceptance of reality, past and present. This seems to me to be the territory on which the interminable therapies are operating. Often it is easier for the patient to keep the therapy stuck and the therapist impotent or "bad" than to face the pain of reality.

Some of the dynamics that I have been describing have been present in aspects of the therapy with a patient whom I shall call "Mr N".

MR N

Mr N has been coming for therapy for seven years, three times weekly for most of that time. He is 36 years old. He was born into a working-class family in the north of England and was the oldest of three siblings: he had a sister six years younger and a brother eight years younger. He describes a close relationship with his mother until his sister was born, but after this point what he mostly remembers is incidents where he would be beaten by his mother with a cricket bat. His father was usually not there when these incidents happened, but when he was, he did sometimes intervene. Early on in the therapy, these actions by his father were described with a self-satisfied grin and a comment that he could twist his father around his little finger.

Although I was quite horrified by what were described as violent and sadistic attacks by Mr N's mother, in monitoring my feelings I concluded that my reaction was one that stemmed entirely from myself—that is, at this early point in the therapy there was no projection into me of pain or anger from the patient. This alerted me to the fact that for Mr N there was no object available for projecting into and that we were up against a profound failure in containment. Quite a lot later I understood that when, quite regularly and untypically for me, I found my thoughts drifting off when Mr N was talking about apparently quite ordinary but in no way boring topics, I was being affected by Mr N's own annihilation of some of his past traumatic experiences. As we have become more in touch with the reality of the experiences and feelings, I have stopped drifting off. In time, I also connected the drifting off and Mr N's tendency to annihilate bad objects with the way he seemed to deny the existence of his siblings. Although he talked about the birth of his sister, for years I did not know of the existence of the younger brother, and both siblings would disappear altogether from his descriptions of family life, as if they truly did not exist.

Another prominent countertransference reaction was a sort of distaste I experienced at Mr N's obvious pleasure and satisfaction as he described these beatings and the way in which he boasted about them and showed off his bruises at school, even though I was aware of this as his inevitable defence in attempting to triumph over the trauma of being beaten by his mother. I felt this reaction of mine reflected also Mr N's healthy awareness of the perversity of this behaviour, since although there were clearly severe difficulties, Mr N could often elicit caring responses from me, from which I inferred healthy good internal objects that could at times exist in an undamaged state. On the other hand, I gathered from a dream, in which Mr N *threw off his dirty and soiled clothes, had a bath, and walked off with a "social worker" type*, that Mr N, unsurprisingly, wanted me to rescue him in an omnipotent way from his past without having to come to terms with the pain and rage of it.

Mr N had come to therapy after the end of a homosexual liaison that had been characterized quite frequently by sadomasochistic violence, both emotional and physical. Finally, he had been left. During the relationship, Mr N had been very attached to this partner, who could, at good times, love him and support him. Although Mr N's suicidal feelings were angry for two years after this loss, and, again, I could not be used as an object to project into, his responses made me realize that he had a strong capacity for love, albeit in a narcissistic and unseparated way. He could feel pain about this partner that he had never felt about his mother. However, during this beginning period of the therapy, he acted out continually, in drinking regularly to stupefaction, in sexual seductions of married women, all the while coming to tell me of these episodes with the perverse sense of triumph that made me aware that part of this behaviour was intended as an attack on me by "proving" that I was useless and had not made him better. After about 18 months of Mr N telling me he did not want to come, that he did not need it, and that he was only here for his friends—whilst never missing a session and always arriving on time—he settled down into a pattern that continued for a few years and can still re-emerge in times of stress.

This pattern consisted in my being subtly invited to be the attacking mother by means of Mr N's intensely provocative and perverse behaviour. Sometimes Mr N could be sensitive and apparently hard-working in the therapy, although I think this could only happen when his own overwhelmingly violent feelings were totally split off and annihilated. But at those times I felt we could work together, and I felt we both learnt more about his internal world, which was full of confusion. However, whenever there was a "good" session in terms of a sense of contact being established, I was treated in the following session to behaviour that I found quite unbearable. There was a tricky, triumphing atmosphere where everything I said was attended to apparently seriously, but in reality was treated

with a response that I experienced as a contemptuous, belit-
tling, triumphing annihilation of my efforts to interpret, reach,
and stay in contact with a healthy part of him that did not want
to be like that. These early attempts of mine were unsuccessful,
and the perverse masquerade tended to be intensified.

At this point, I mostly found it impossible to hide my feelings
of annoyance and sometimes anger. Nevertheless, I persisted
in interpreting that he had succeeded in making me get angry
and criticize him, which felt like his mother beating him, because he was so afraid of becoming dependent on me. I was
also aware that I was being made to feel so hopeless and impotent because Mr N had split off the terrible hopelessness and
despair in relation to his mother and, specifically, the helpless-
ness in being unable to defend himself against his mother's
violence. He had clearly, at some point, begun to provoke her
to attack him, in order to feel in control of the situation, which
he did with a masochistic triumph. I wondered if Mr N's rage
was rooted in an earlier trauma of infantile non-containment,
and whether it was this early fragmented state that was expelled violently into his mother, as it was into me, which his
mother could not stand and which led later on to the beatings.
In the transference, he was trying to continue with this strat-
egy.

My sense of impotence was also linked with Mr N's healthy
part, which was also completely dominated by the pathological organization and was therefore also impotent. This situation continued for a long while, where nothing seemed to
change, or if it did, it seemed to be for the worse, and often I
felt it was in reality truly hopeless.

In retrospect, I think that the only thing that helped Mr N was
that I survived and did not throw him out. The fact that he
came absolutely regularly and sometimes confessed that on
occasion he made a special detour to drive past my house
made me aware that there was something in him that was
aware of what must have felt like an overwhelming and fright-
eningly regressive dependency. I noted that sessions that
seemed to be filled with Mr N's perverse triumph increased in

frequency as we approached breaks. Gradually I was able to contain more and more the underlying rage, pain, and the terror he felt that he would fall apart if he allowed himself to be dependent, which was consequent on allowing me to be a helpful figure.

In time, I became an object into whom the rage could be projected. This was also difficult in the countertransference because of its overwhelming nature. It also appeared to be very primitive and linked with early omnipotence, as it arose in connection with developing conscious awareness in Mr N of feeling dependent on me. I formed the hypothesis that Mr N's problem with his mother had indeed started early on in his life, and that the traumatic beatings had revived an earlier trauma. I tried to interpret both what I have called the "psychotic" rage, Mr N's hatred of dependency and of me as someone who could help and thus aroused it, and also his realistic rage at having a mother who did not appear to have been at all able to help him with early, overwhelming anxieties that seemed mainly linked with loss of containment. I felt that she must have been a mother who could not allow a maternal reverie, who could not stand her baby's frustrations, and who always tried to gratify him. If she could not, she attacked him for his neediness. There seemed to be an internal situation of complete lack of separation, presumably brought about mainly by the wholesale projection of Mr N's primitive destructive feelings into his mother. In reality she appeared to have reenacted these in the beatings. On her own part, she seemed to have needed to be in total control. Now that Mr N is adult, she has reappeared, when he visits his parents, as a quiet, somewhat withdrawn figure who tries to help in Mr N's problems with his father.

Gradually, the powerful rage has diminished, and Mr N has become aware of becoming panicky when he felt I was out of reach, that when he starts to feel his dependence on me, he becomes very frightened. He fears loss of control and of becoming disintegrated. Occasionally, he touches briefly on feelings linked with his mother's attacks, and the pain feels truly unbearable. I am aware he is now using me as someone he can project into as a form of communication.

Although the therapy can still be very difficult, and no doubt will continue to be so for some time, I believe that Mr N falls into the group of patients whose destructiveness was constituted less by death-instinct forces, with excessive psychotic rage; they are, rather, defensive against the terrors of disintegration linked with early problems with containment. His capacity to retain good objects and what is emerging as the beginnings of a true capacity for love and gratitude has helped him to make use of what I could offer.

Conclusion

In this chapter I have tried to illuminate aspects of the debate surrounding the relative importance of intra-psychic and external factors in the formation of personality. These will, of course, differ in any given individual; but I note that Kleinian thinking has developed since its earliest beginnings to a more realistic appreciation of external influences, or perhaps to a greater willingness to include them in the analysis of what are often complex interrelationships between internal objects and between internal and external objects. This, to my mind, makes Kleinian theory more fully object-related.

The universality of phantasy as underlying all conscious thought and feeling is accepted, but I have argued that failures in the psychic environment of the child, often linked with inadequate containment or other failures that can have a traumatizing effect, also require interpretation. I have also tried to disentangle different aspects of the rage that can emerge in a therapy, interpretation of which, it is hoped, can help in the containment of a patient during what can be a very difficult time for both patient and therapist.

CHAPTER FOUR

"Turning a blind eye": misrepresentation and the denial of life events

Mary Adams

A patient, Mr H, would often preface what he was going to say with the comment: "I know this is not really the case, but. . . ." He would then describe to me his own view of things that he knew other people would consider untrue. He was a bright young man in his mid-twenties, highly articulate and already successful in his career. However, he felt endlessly tormented by his view of the world, driven to violent rage by it, and unable to give it up. He seemed caught in a claustrum world where his only pleasure was in sadism and triumph. It was a world constructed to defend against the kinds of emotional experiences—painful or joyful—that were out of his control. It was a way, ultimately, I believe, of defending against unresolved oedipal guilt.

For the first two years of Mr H's life, as well as looking after him and his older brother, his mother was caring for her dying sister. Extreme rivalry for the mother's attention developed between the two brothers, which persisted throughout their teens and led to worrying physical violence between them. Although guarded about this, Mr H described "whole holidays being ruined" by the viciousness of their fights. Tragically, during Mr H's adolescence his father became ill with a degenerating illness and remained in a nursing home until his death.

Although he sought therapy at the point when his father's death seemed imminent, Mr H attached no importance to this. He felt, he said, as though his father had died years before and had never really been a presence in his life anyway. What concerned him were his intense and violent feelings towards his girlfriend and his brother. While his father's illness was uppermost in my mind, Mr H felt that the real trauma in his life was shortly after his father first became ill, when his girlfriend had become pregnant and had to have an abortion. He described in dramatic detail the shame he felt at this, particularly at the fact that he had "turned away from her and tried to deny that it had happened". From that point he seems to have felt the accusing eyes of the world on him and lived in fear of being exposed and condemned for his "irresponsibility and cowardice".

Clearly, getting his girlfriend pregnant was a difficult and frightening experience for him. However, the depth of self-condemnation he expressed and the way he consequently threw himself into his studies had more the feel of fear and guilt towards a damaged and dying father. Mr H's continued conviction that it was his brother, not his father, who was his rival, taken together with his belief that it was his girlfriend's abortion rather than his father's illness that dramatically changed his life, conveyed a powerful message that this was an emotional area that could not be touched. What I want to focus on is the paralysing effect that I believe this kind of denial had on his emotional growth as well as on the therapy.

In his psychoanalytic study of the Sophocles plays *Oedipus the King* and *Oedipus at Colonus*, John Steiner discusses two different ways that Oedipus tried to deal with reality. He describes how in the first play Oedipus attempts to retreat from the truth by *turning a blind eye*, and Steiner argues that Oedipus both *"knew and did not know the truth of what he was doing"*. In the second play Oedipus is seen as expressing contempt for the truth by *turning to omnipotence and self-righteousness*, retreating from contact with inner reality, and abandoning human values (Steiner, 1993, p. 116; italics added).

Mr H seemed to alternate between these two ways of denying reality. Both ways rely on what Money-Kyrle termed "*misrepresentation*"—namely, lying to oneself (Money-Kyrle, 1968, p. 417). The attempt to lie to oneself about reality inevitably interferes with the ability to recognize, value and accept the "facts of life"—specifically, one's dependence on internal and external objects, generational differences, the creativity of the parental couple, and finally the "inevitability of time and ultimately of death" (Money-Kyrle, 1971, p. 103–106). With Mr H, I was often left feeling how tragic it was that, in having to misrepresent reality to himself, he was left blind to the good will that existed towards him and to how human and understandable the feelings are of rivalry and exclusion that dominated his life.

Turning a blind eye

Mr H came into therapy plagued with images of his girlfriend having sex with other lovers. Rather than trying to rid himself of the images, however, he persistently goaded her into providing him with details of previous affairs—details that left him feeling inadequate by comparison. Apart from the obvious masochism involved, once he had the details, he felt fully justified in condemning her as a "slut who could never be trusted". He would become consumed with thoughts of her having "fantastic sex" with other men and would work himself up into a violent rage. This was truly an obsession with him, one that regularly filled his mind and kept him blind to the reality that she was in fact faithfully devoted to him. It was as though her very existence as separate from him represented a betrayal, and only in death would she be his alone. (For a discussion of the link between narcissism and jealous rage, see Fisher, 1999.)

As soon as he had sufficiently "disposed" of his girlfriend in his thoughts, he would then move on to someone else who elicited rage in him, most often describing his brother's "unforgivable behaviour" towards him when they were younger. The fact that they were now both adults with separate lives and hardly ever saw each other made no difference and gives an idea of his ability to misrepresent the reality that time had passed since then.

Mr H's inner world was one of schoolboy one-upmanship in which you are either bullied or the bully—you are the one who counts or you are no one. There was no escape, no benign powerful figure to intervene. Perhaps most importantly, there was no forgiveness. It was a harsh, rigidly constructed, hierarchical world.

> In a typical dream, *Mr H was with a group of schoolmates, one of whom stood up and announced they were all displeased with him and disowning him. It was a sea of dark faces condemning him. He felt resigned to the inevitability of this and the humiliation.*

As long as he is resigned ultimately to have to face condemnation, Mr H can have little drive for understanding or developing concern for his object. Instead, everything is oriented to getting through the moment, relentlessly hounded by fear of condemnation and desperate to avoid it. Joan Riviere describes this essentially hopeless state of mind in her paper on the "Negative Therapeutic Reaction":

> All his efforts to put things right never succeed *enough*; he can only pacify his internal persecutors for a time, fob them off, feed them with sops, "keep them going"; and so he "keeps things going" . . . and *postpones* the crash, the day of reckoning and judgement. [Riviere, 1936, p. 314]

What Mr H brought to me were the raging inner battles with perceived rivals and betraying mothers and his wish to exact revenge. The only sense of a future was in some imagined final triumph and punishment of other people's wrong doings.

> In a recurring dream, *he and his brother are in a fight to the death. He fights with all his strength, beats his brother to the ground and feels good because this time he wins.*

The dream felt good, he said, because in reality he always had to back off. My sense is, however, that he did *not* back off. His story is one of always having tried to push himself forward and "eliminate" the competition.

Self-adulation as an attack on coupling

Mr H said that as a child he was always either annoyingly trying to push himself into the middle of everything to make sure he was noticed and admired or he was escaping into a world of his own. Neither of these states allowed him to notice or credit how much he actually might be valued and cared about. And it was still the case that no amount of adulation actually helped when he was caught between these two isolating ways of being, ways in which he felt profoundly unlikeable.

"Pushing himself into the middle" was something he still felt driven to, and had the quality of a child pushing himself between the parents to prevent any coupling from taking place, wishing to deny his position as the child. Mr H saw it in terms of "seeking adulation": "When I arrive at work each day", he explained, "I cannot just go to my office and get on with things. Instead, I have to spend ages making sure I have a chat with everyone from the porter on up, being sure to amuse them and have them admire me." As long as he could keep people admiring him, it seemed, he was both keeping them from being with others and postponing the condemnation to come.

Although successful in his career, he feared he could not live up to the expectations he had created. He felt he was "living a lie". If he did not need all the flattery and adulation, he said, he would prefer a simple, routine job. As it was, he lived in fear of either being exposed as not being up to the job or of having his childish, querulous, or violent self spilling out and ruining everything. I tried to point out to him the link between his inability to accept the reality of his parental couple as a couple, his own relation to them as the child, and his hatred of any evidence that he was anything less than adult.

Misrepresentation as a psychic retreat

In the analytic work, Mr H was quickly able to acknowledge how much his feelings of jealousy must have to do with his early experience and his wish to have his mother to himself. We could even marvel together at his choice of girlfriend, who, being older

than him, "confident and sexy" and someone who had undoubtedly had previous lovers, would be seen by him as much more
the "unfaithful mother" than the "young, virginal peasant girl"
of his sexual fantasies. Nor did he hesitate to admit that, in reality,
his girlfriend was devoted and faithful to him. But still he clung
to his own fantasy version of her infidelity. This was one of the
most striking features of the denial—namely, his ability to hold
two contradictory versions of reality simultaneously. The benefit
of therapy, it seemed, was that he could tell me the details of his
jealous fantasies and not have to put his girlfriend through so
much heartache. Giving up the fantasies, however, did not seem
to be an option.

In his book, *Psychic Retreats*, John Steiner describes how in
most such retreats a special relationship with reality is established
in which *"reality is neither fully accepted nor completely disavowed"*,
and he sees this as "a perverse mechanism designed to keep the
patient's idealized and persecutory versions of himself and his
objects apart" (Steiner, 1993, p. 88). He refers to Freud's 1927 paper on fetishism, which discusses ways in which the child deals
with facts of life that are difficult to accept. Significantly for this
chapter, two of the examples Freud gives involve the inability of
the patients (both male) to accept their father's early death. Freud
says:

> It was only one current in their mental life that had not recog-
> nized their father's death; there was another current, which
> took full account of that fact. The attitude which fitted in with
> the wish and the attitude which fitted in with the reality ex-
> isted side by side. [Freud, 1927e, p. 156]

Steiner maintains that "it is such misrepresentations of reality
that are the chief obstacle when we attempt to help the patient
come to terms with the reality of loss". He goes on to describe the
situation in which, as treatment proceeds and the patient gains
insight, he or she can no longer keep the opposing versions of
reality apart:

> A stage is commonly reached when he can no longer maintain
> the split but does not yet feel able to tolerate the reality which
> integration brings. Perverse mechanisms then become accen-
> tuated and may lead to a stalemate if the patient is rescued by

a pathological organisation of the personality which provides
a retreat or shelter in which the perverse reconciliation of op-
posites is allowed. [Steiner, 1993, p. 94]

I believe it was this kind of stalemate that I reached with Mr H
after two years of treatment as he found his own version of reality
less and less tenable.

Misrepresentation of intercourse

A retreat from reality can sometimes mean a retreat to an anal
world in which differences are denied and control of the object is
paramount. Furthermore, "living a lie" and in fear of being found
out restricts the spontaneity and risk-taking essential to real intercourse within the analytic relationship as well as in his personal
life.

Mr H sought therapy genuinely worried about his potential for
destroying everything and losing everyone. However, we were
immediately faced with his wish not to know. From our first meeting he was telling me what he could not do and did not want to
know. For example, he told me that he did not want to find out
that he is homosexual. And he could not make any of the times I
offered him, even though they had been made clear before we
met. It seemed I was to fit in with his busy schedule.

Following our first (four-week) break in the therapy, Mr H
chose to go away for another five weeks. This same clear message
that he could not bear there to be any difference between us and
that he was to be the one to control what happened was repeated
with predictable regularity. It was the message when he cancelled
sessions or came late after weekend breaks. It was the message
when I announced my holiday breaks, and he immediately announced that he would be away before or after that. Despite the
regularity of this response, he continued to take me by surprise, as
it was in marked contrast to the intense involvement he conveyed
in the sessions.

He invariably arrived late, huffing and puffing as though it
had been a monumental task getting to his session. Once on the
couch, however, he seemed settled in forever. Always earnest and
hardworking, he conveyed that I was to take things seriously with

him, follow his lead, and restrict my interventions. The only thoughts he wanted me to have were those that came from him. In his view, any other thoughts that I might have had would have been from previous patients, evidence that there had been others before him. He would perform impressively and entertainingly, filling the time with the elaborate detail of the workings of his mind and creating a sense of intimacy between us, a pseudo-intimacy based more on a fantasy of our being the same than on any real emotional intercourse. To use Edna O'Shaughnessy's concepts of "enclaves" and "excursions", it was as though he were set on drawing me into a circumscribed enclave of over-closeness and then leading me off on tantalizing excursions, both modes of relating being designed to avoid real emotional engagement and facing reality (O'Shaughnessy, 1992, pp. 604–605).

At the end of each session, when I would indicate it was time, he would seem somehow stunned and would sigh and rub his eyes before reluctantly getting up. His departure was often dismaying, as he would fix me with a contemptuous look or become clumsy and in a mess.

An account he once gave of a meeting he had at work seemed similar to his sessions with me:

"You see", he said, "in the past I would have been one of two ways. Either I would not have said a word, felt like I didn't exist, and allowed myself to be bullied. Or, I would have become loud, offensive and bellicose. At this morning's meeting, it was a set-up for all sorts of rivalry and competition, too many egos, a lot at stake. What happens now is different. I started off quiet and then gradually began to contribute more and more. The more people liked what I had to say, the more I liked the feeling, the attention, and the more I came to dominate the meeting. Then I cracked a joke, and it went down well, so I cracked another and then another. But then I felt unable to let go and let anyone else have a say."

Feeling unable to let go and let anyone else have a say, wanting to dominate and be admired leaves him little or nothing of real value or meaning to take with him. Either he is the one on stage or he does not exist. In his contempt, I am reduced to being of no importance to him. It is as though he were identified with a mother who had to fit him in, along with all the other demands being made on her, rather than a mother with whom he had a unique and meaningful relationship.

In the lead-up to our second holiday break, he was struggling with pressure from his girlfriend to make a solid commitment to her as she wanted children. Rather than focus on the emotional commitment involved, he became preoccupied with images of children mocking and humiliating him. When he returned after the break, however, he told me his partner was pregnant. While I felt shocked by this news, he seemed indifferent. He said that in his indecisiveness he had allowed it to happen but found that in some ways he liked it. Having her "on a ball and chain" he had less need to feel jealous. He even began talking about their having a second child. I interpreted his wish to sever any emotional contact between his partner and baby by keeping her constantly pregnant, producing more babies.

At this time, and six months into the therapy, Mr H's father died. Despite having been with his father during the week before, he hardly mentioned it. It was as though it had not happened, although my countertransference once again seemed to resonate with an anxiety and sadness he could not allow. Similarly, his dismissal of what his pregnant partner and now his mother were going through at this time—his annoyance with them, in fact—was disturbing. His partner was "becoming dowdy, losing her figure and her sex appeal". His mother in her grief was scorned as "getting old and repeating herself". When he talked this way, it was hard to picture how he was when actually with the people close to him, and it was often only by understanding the defensive nature of this apparent disregard for his objects, how he would idealize and denigrate them simultaneously, that I could listen sympathetically.

Ronald Britton describes how such patients feel they cannot afford to know the reality of either their internal or external objects as they expect to find them irreparably damaged, devastated or horrifying:

> They seek refuge in a state of unreality that characterises all their relationships. The "blind but seeing eye" is directed not

only outward but inward so that it is not only the things of this world that are known and not known, but also all thoughts *and* feelings. In such persons their external perceptions lack significance and their inner experience lacks substance. [Britton, 1994a, p. 366]

At the same time, however, I believe Mr H was occasionally in touch with a part of himself that does value what others can give him. But it was a part, that presented him with the kind of depressive pain and guilt that he seemed ill-equipped to bear. Far from being contemptuous of all intimacy, he was increasingly bringing the pain of feeling caught between his wish for intimacy and his warring self. Caught in this dilemma, he would turn to fantasies to try to escape his need for others:

In one he is a sports hero, the best there is and everyone is admiring and in awe of him. This is the "extrovert" him, he said. There is no competition involved, in fact no one else exists. In another he cuts off from the world completely, raising barriers around himself. "It is like going back into the womb or shutting myself away", he explained, "so that I can't see anyone and no one can stir up feelings".

These two states also seem to describe his alternating kinds of behaviour with me, one moment working hard to seduce me into his self-idealization, entertaining me with his colourful and dramatic descriptions, and the next turning in on himself, cutting me off, and disappearing.

The delusional retreat

Given his kind of thinking, it is not surprising that Mr H often talked about feeling trapped. Sometimes it was about situations such as being in a relationship and having a new baby, but more often it was about his own tormenting thoughts—thoughts that he produced incessantly, with clockwork regularity. When once I wondered with him about his inability to let go of his jealous thoughts, he responded, "No, it's as though they hug me". "You make them sound almost comfortable", I replied. "Well, 'grip' then", he said, disgruntled.

No matter how persecuting the images were, the feelings that they produced were familiar, predictable, and under his control. There was a perverse kind of safety to them and a fetishistic quality in the way he was constantly working to keep the misrepresentation alive.

In one session I said, "One of the problems with holding on to such a tormenting view of the world is that it deprives you of feeling pleasure in your life, such as anticipating the birth of your first child." "I know no other way of thinking", he replied. "I don't know what pleasure is. I can never relax. Other people are able to feel the warm glow of pleasure of being in a relationship, expecting a child. That's just not something I know." This kind of despairing resignation to his fate seemed to contain the message that this way of being was not something he was about to give up. He seemed trapped in the kind of delusional pathological organization described by Herbert Rosenfeld (1971a), Edna O'Shaughnessy (1981), and John Steiner (1993), among others.

> The refuge can be a terrifying one but nevertheless is turned to as if the patient is addicted to it. . . . Once established, this type of retreat is very difficult to relinquish partly because the grievance provides a focus and purpose for the patient and partly because of other sources of gratification such as those related to triumph and to masochism. In some cases the patient appears to "feed" or "nurse" the grievance and gets gratification by "keeping old wounds open". [Steiner, 1993, p. 76]

Mr H's detailed descriptions of his various inner torments, although in one sense highly appropriate material for therapy, were like the kind of acting out described by Donald Meltzer as characteristic of the pseudo-mature patient, designed to control tightly what happens in sessions and to elicit praise rather than interpretation and understanding. Meltzer describes the subtle pressure put on the therapist to "join in the idealization of the pseudo-maturity" (Meltzer, 1992, p. 17). There were times when I felt pleased by how well we were working together and what a good patient he was, but then I realized how cleverly he would steer things to maintain the *status quo*. Betty Joseph talks about the way defences are mobilized at the moment of nearly having to face psychic reality:

> [The patient] believes that [he] wants to be understood but [in his omnipotence] cannot tolerate not knowing. [His] aggression is mobilised when this omniscient balance is disturbed by my interpretations; then placating is mobilised to deal with this, as [he] unconsciously tries to draw me into [his] defensive organisation and keep us in perpetual agreement. [Joseph, 1983, p. 294]

When once I suggested that he was filling the sessions with his usual topics so that nothing more painful might arise, he responded with indignation and hurt: "What could be more painful than the mental torment I am bringing?" He then tried, in vain, to think of what he might be avoiding. I think his shocked reaction gives a sense of the power of the delusional organization as a defence in the way it clings to a belief that nothing could be worse than the pain already experienced—while at another level fearing a worse fate if reality is really to be faced.

The perverse retreat

In his attempts at self-adulation Mr H would, as I have indicated, escape into fantasies or daydreams of a sexual liaison with a young virginal woman—fantasies that seem to defend against oedipal jealousies. "She will have had no previous lovers, and there will be no competition", he stressed. A more debilitating defence against oedipal reality, however, is the establishment of the "perverse retreat", as described by Chasseguet-Smirgel (1985) and Steiner (1993). Both talk about the rejection of the genital universe for an anal one in which differences between the sexes and between generations do not exist.

In a rare comment about his father's death, Mr H said that his regret was that he was never able to show his father that he was his "equal". Perhaps far more painful would be to regret not having his father proud of him, for example, which would acknowledge the difference in age as well as the significant familial relationship between them. Mostly, however, his father was ignored as if the generational differences were non-existent or at least insignificant. As Chasseguet-Smirgel observes:

> The abolition of differences prevents psychic suffering at all levels: feelings of inadequacy, castration, loss, absence and death no longer exist. [Chasseguet-Smirgel, 1985, p. 6]

Two dreams in particular seem to convey his use of retreat into an anal world:

> In one *he was having a torrid affair with a woman at work whom he had not much noticed. It was all secrets and hotel-rooms. Then he went to the lavatory. He had been constipated, and this felt a great relief.*

In the session we agreed that he seemed to see therapy as a "toilet" for relief. In terms of a retreat into an anal world it would seem that the "torrid affair" is associated with constipation, as though the "affair" were in "secret" places of his body and with his own faeces. His relief is to flush the feelings down the toilet.

> In the second dream, brought before a holiday break, *he needed to go to the lavatory and he went downstairs, but there was a queue of people waiting. He continued on down looking into the different rooms in the building. It seemed to be all baby-changing-rooms. Then there was one with a group of ten beautiful young women. They thought he looked lost and took him in, looked after him, made him feel wonderful. Feeling much better in himself, he continued on down. At one point he was in a wonderful sauna-room with beautiful wood panelling. When he looked into another room, a friend was there with her two young children. She looked shocked, not recognizing him, and went to protect them. A midwife was waiting. He felt he should not have been looking in. He continued on down and successfully found a lavatory.*

Mr H linked this dream with the fact that my consulting-room is in a tall building and that the lavatory had been occupied by another patient the previous day. I interpreted his being "taken in" by the ten beautiful women as his use of sexual fantasy to avoid the pain of separation after the session and during the coming break. The being "taken in" could even be a pun acknowledging some awareness that he fools himself with his masturbatory fantasy. Following Meltzer (1992), the *ten* beautiful women would seem to represent Mr H's ten fingers and an escape into anal masturbation—a state of mind of being the one in control. Masturbation in this sense is described as "any stimulation designed to induce a state of omnipotence" (Meltzer, 1971, p. 210). This can be seen as Mr H's way of coping while being made to wait, either during the holiday break or while his mother is preoccupied with a queue of others: father and brother, aunt or other babies.

The baby-changing-rooms seemed to relate to what goes on in the other compartments of the mother's body, and there was a sense that he is a threat to these other babies with his murderous wishes. Baby-changing-rooms imply dirty nappies, and one gets a picture of the baby in his idealized cot (beautiful wood panelling) being made to wait and discovering that he can control his own faeces and get physical pleasure from doing so. Meltzer suggests that:

> Entry into projective identification is a ubiquitous phenomenon in early childhood mainly instituted during conflicts over excretory processes and implemented through phantasies of penetrating masturbatory activities, especially anal masturbation. [Meltzer, 1992, p. 118]

Particularly striking is the image of the therapist as "waiting midwife". Perhaps internally Mr H was developing a sense of the therapist/midwife in a helpful role and his new thoughts as being a creation of the therapy. Perhaps he was valuing her experience and containing function, even if at another level he was reducing her to a servant taking orders as the new thoughts emerge from him alone.

The denial of birth and death

For many patients the death of a parent or the birth of a child are key events that allow for new growth and understanding in their lives. They provide a sense of "moving on" in life, "growing up", acquiring a new, more mature identity—all of which would involve a process of mourning. For Mr H, however, these events seemed to pass him by.

In the first session after the birth of his child, Mr H made me wait for most of the session before mentioning it, and even then I was given little detail. He also seemed to be turning away from his girlfriend. I commented: "It is as though her body has become indistinguishable from your mother's, and you can only see all the rival men and babies that have been inside her." He referred to his wife and mother as "old and needy". "You make them sound like used goods", I said. He latched onto this, embellishing his condemnation of them: "I get filled with indignation if other people need me", he said, "outraged if they are no longer there servicing me and I'm expected to service them." Mr H's ability to reduce those people most important to him to the realm of "servicing" slaves and prostitutes was perhaps an indication of his unconscious fear of losing them to a fate of deterioration like his father or his aunt.

Meltzer points out that the damaged object does not merely lose the qualities of "goodness, age, beauty, strength, and contentment" that make up its parental character—they are replaced by persecutory qualities. Through sadistic attack on the object it becomes "old, ugly, functionless and resentful" (Meltzer, 1971, pp. 212–213).

In a subsequent session Mr H became weighed down and worried. He could only see "a long dark tunnel ahead, with no light at the end", and I found my mind filled with an image of his father's illness. It was as though, unconsciously identified with his father's long, slow death, he was not allowed a life himself and had split off the unbearable feelings and projected them into me. The denigration of his objects denies the fact of life of goodness coming from the object. In addition, he also denies to himself the reality of mortality, birth, and ageing. In his inner world, birth seems to be equated with the appearance of mother's other babies who will compete with him, while death seems to be equated with murdering one's competitors. This leaves him in a joyless, static world, unable to "move on" emotionally. For as long as life events have to be blocked from having any real meaning, there can be no learning from experience. In the therapy, Mr H would "practice", as he puts it, how other people might view a situation, but any experience of direct emotional engagement with me would be followed by his immediately cutting off in some way.

A hint of what his father's death might mean was expressed in his telling me that he felt unable to read the letters of condolence. He had to push them away, otherwise he would have "cried uncontrollably and been speechless in front of everyone". Even at moments when he gets close to his grief, we find him in front of a hostile or mocking crowd in his mind. Once he had to go to a memorial service for a colleague. "What happened", he told me, "showed how many defences I have. They get stripped away at such occasions, and I find myself in tears. All my life I seem to go between feeling either vengeance and violence or tearful, weak, and fragile." He continued: "I thought about my father and know that's sitting there. But it doesn't feel like it's that. It feels like my brother."

This had been a session with genuine contact between us, so I should not have been surprised when he did not appear the following day—a Friday—and I heard nothing until he came for his session the following Tuesday. He apologized. What happened was typical, he said, and had to do with his being late everywhere. He had set off for his session but found himself "gridlocked" in traffic. When he did finally get here, he just "froze" and felt unable to come in. Instead, he spent the time sitting in the car trying to understand what was happening. He identified four stages:

In *stage one* he feels resentful at having to leave where he is. He knows he is procrastinating and that he will be late, but he ignores the consequences. In *stage two* he is on his way and busily trying to think of an excuse for being late, even though it means lying. *Stage three*, "the worst point", is the moment of confrontation when he meets the person's eyes, gives his excuse, and faces their anger. In *stage four*, if his excuse is accepted and no anger shown, then he feels a reprieve. He added that the way he froze on the Friday reminded him of when he was 16 and had to face his girlfriend's father's rage when she had to have an abortion. He felt like "the scum of the earth", he knew he was to blame and had no excuse.

Mr H's wish to "stay where he is" can be heard as the addictive pull of the psychic retreat. Emerging from the retreat, he faces exposure of his fraudulence (the lies, the misrepresentation) and a confrontation with reality (the eyes and a different point of view). Since I represented for him the aspects of reality that he could not face, I was the one he must control and keep away.

I think with this incident we were beginning to reach the point to which Steiner refers in which the possibility of keeping the opposing views of reality apart was becoming more difficult for Mr H. Once I said to him, "It is striking how clearly you describe your own tormenting view of things as well as what you know to be the reality. In fact, you seem to keep the two separate from each other, as though that feels somehow safer." He tried to think through for himself what might happen if he brought the two sides together. "I suppose I would have to accept the impossibility of my infantile wishes, that I was never going to be the best, the only one", he said.

The unbearable oedipal reality

I believe Mr H's "four stages" can be seen as a picture of how he was constantly thwarting any move from the paranoid–schizoid to the depressive position in order to avoid being confronted by his own emerging conscience and the pain of all he must mourn. The image of his "turning away" when confronted by his girlfriend's father seems a turning-away from reality to avoid feelings of pain and guilt, the girlfriend's accusing father having come to represent his own dead internalized father as persecutor (Klein, 1955, p. 161). For as long as Mr H has no concept of forgiveness and understanding and merely deals in accusation and counter-accusation, feelings of guilt are intolerable. Instead, he must rely on the use of projective identification, splitting off the feelings into internal and external objects and then punishing or rejecting them. He feels so much better, he says, now that he stays away from his brother—"staying away" being his only way of feeling better. As we have seen, this pattern was repeated regularly in the relationship with me as he found reasons for "staying away" from sessions, particularly before and after breaks. These were occasions, of course, when unconsciously he could picture me as finding something or someone else more interesting than he.

What was trapping him in particular was the difficulty in facing oedipal reality. While his father's importance is denied and the couple that he is attacking is his mother and his brother, the reality of the parental couple cannot be faced. His mother and brother are not a "parental" couple. This constitutes, in fact, an attack on the reality of the generational divide between his parents and him and his brother. Similarly, the generational divide represented in his being the patient and my being the therapist he found intolerable. I could absent myself when I chose, but for him to absent himself was like being the delinquent child.

For Mr H, it is as though fantasy became reality when his murderous wishes towards his father coincided with the father becoming terminally ill. Unable to contain such trauma and guilt, he then had to create his own delusional reality, distorting the truth, "living a lie", and blocking any grieving process.

As Steiner (1993) and others emphasize, only by being faced with clear parent/child boundaries and a true parental couple in the transference can a move to the depressive position take place. And it is not until loss and mourning can be experienced in the containment of therapy and parts of the self begin to be reintegrated that Mr H will have the strength to mourn his father's death. Perhaps only then would he be able to see his father's illness as a tragedy to be grieved for rather than something for which he must feel shame.

Mr H's ability to observe with me the emotional trap in which he found himself seemed impressive and hopeful. "How do I unpack all of this?" he asked. "Maybe it is more a question of how you let go of it", I responded. "Well, that's a good question. I seem addicted to it", he said. It was another of those moments of emotional contact between us, and perhaps the hope it inspired in me was an indication that he would find it too much.

Unfortunately, soon after this and following another summer break, he wrote, asking to reduce his sessions from three times a week to once a fortnight, quite aware that I would not be happy with this. I replied that we needed to talk it over, but I had no response. It was as though he had begun to allow the experience of a good object but that this brought with it the fear of more real emotional engagement than he could bear. As a result, I was left feeling suspended between two opposing versions of reality: the therapy was both over and not over. We were "gridlocked", it seemed, over the patient's need to misrepresent life events.

CHAPTER FIVE

Tolerating emotional knowledge

Stanley Ruszczynski

The primary task of psychoanalytic clinicians is to listen to and observe everything that is going on in the consulting-room: in the patient, in the therapist, and in the relationship between the two. This is usually referred to by the concept of the total situation of the transference (Joseph, 1985; Klein, 1952). This primary task also requires that from time to time we say something to our patient about what we have heard or observed. This usually comes in the form of a description, which, if we have listened and observed sufficiently acutely, will inevitably include meaning or interpretation. Understanding or insight may emerge.

This clinical stance has long informed clinical practice. Freud recommended that we listen to our patients with free-floating attention; Sandler advocates free-floating responsiveness; Bion tells us to listen with negative capability, with no memory or desire; Betty Joseph promotes a detailed tracking of every moment in the session; Dennis Carpy and Irma Brenman-Pick (amongst others) describe, respectively, the necessity of tolerating and then working through in the countertransference.

There is probably little argument with these clinical parameters, all of which address us in relation to our clinical receptivity. However, psychoanalysis has developed as a result of the constant interplay between clinical practice and theoretical understanding, because we all need to have some sort of theoretical construct in our minds, which meets with what we hear and observe and helps us to organize our experience. In addition to our receptivity, therefore, we are required to have available an active mind that might process our experiences. Bion writes that such organizing of our experience leads to the emergence of what he called a "selected fact"—a sort of meta-observation that links the disparate facts and observations and might result in a comment to the patient or an interpretation. He stresses that "the selected fact is the name of an *emotional* experience, the *emotional* experience of a sense of discovery of coherence" (Bion, 1962b, italics added).

Whatever our theoretical framework might be, our comments and interpretations will only be useful to the patient if they make links between the bewildering variety of material presented to us. To arrive at the "selected fact" that creates a sense of cohesion, we often need to bear long periods of uncertainty, and often confusion and anxiety. This is probably the most difficult aspect of the psychotherapeutic process.

Steiner and Britton (Britton, 1998; Britton & Steiner, 1994) warn us to take care not to confuse the eventual emergence of a "selected fact", which does actually link disparate data together, with what they call an "overvalued idea" offered defensively by the therapist so as to avoid confusion and uncertainty. They suggest that the emergence of the "selected fact", precisely because it does make links, gives coherence and meaning and so produces in the patient the sense of being contained. The emergence of an "overvalued idea", on the other hand, because it makes spurious connections in a defensive attempt to deal with anxiety and fragility, will not be containing, though the patient might collude with the illusion that it is. In a similar way, patients themselves may produce and promote overvalued ideas, sometimes seducing the therapist into compliance and sometimes finding the therapist colluding for his own defensive reasons. Not infrequently, patients overvalue facts rather than attempting the hard work of discovering meaning, which can only be found through the making of links. This is not an uncommon experience.

In this chapter I have tried to write about a particular constellation of ideas that I have found useful in my clinical thinking and practice with individual patients. I have already written about some of these ideas in relation to psychotherapeutic work with couples (Ruszczynski, 1997).

Mrs F

I will start with some material from a patient. Mrs F is American-born but has lived in this country for most of her adult years. She is in her late forties and is employed as a personnel manager. She is married, with three daughters, two grown-up and married, with their own young families, and one in further education. She has, by her account, an interesting and full life.

She came into treatment complaining about unspecific dissatisfactions, periods of depression, outbursts of verbal aggression, and a general feeling of insecurity and lack of fulfilment. In the first session she said, "It is as if I have something in my hands and it then slips out of my fingers. I look around at what I have, I feel very fortunate, and suddenly it all sort of crumbles . . . something goes wrong, and I have nothing. I know. . . . I think I know. . . . that I don't actually lose things, but at the same time I feel as if I do. . . . or at least I think I do."

She settled into intensive therapeutic work quickly and very rarely missed sessions even though she had a busy professional and social life. In the transference, for some time she experienced me as a good object, specifically as someone prepared to be available to her and engage with her. She brought dreams and free-associated to her material without great difficulty. She seemed to have an available and enquiring mind.

However, alongside this at times suspiciously positive atmosphere, there also emerged a quite different dynamic. Mrs F has the most extraordinary capacity for observation: she noticed minor changes in the consulting-room—for example, a book shelved in a different place in my bookcase; she noticed particular verbal expressions I might use, or the detail of my words to end a session. When arriving for the session or when leaving, she noticed the different cars parked outside or near the consulting-room and she noticed various people near the house. She was often acutely sensitive to and accurate about those who might be patients. Sometimes she told me about what she had noticed; at other times, I would later learn that she had withheld her observation with a sense of triumph and glee.

When she is in this acutely watchful state of mind, I often come to feel increasingly uncomfortable: I become aware of being very watchful of myself because I fear that at any moment I might do or say something that she would notice, deeply disapprove of, and seek her revenge. In this state of mind I can feel quite disturbed and not be able to think of much other than this sense of threat to my own survival. Everything she says I find myself treating with suspicion and guardedness. I find myself preoccupied with this sense of danger and become aware of highly paranoid object relationships both internal and external to me.

I have come to realize that before I become consciously aware of my anxieties, the patient and I engage in superficial and spurious work, no doubt as a product of the anxiety that begins to fill the space between us. In this atmosphere Mrs F loses her capacity to symbolize and to think more reflectively (as I eventually do too). She becomes quite concrete in her thinking, and nothing can be explored for its meaning. For example, rather than think about what it meant to her that I had apparently used two different ways of finishing the session on two consecutive days, she simply insists that I confirm that I had done so. That new book in the shelves—she would ask—did I buy it and read it over the weekend or had I simply put it there from elsewhere in my shelves? Any attempts to interpret her intense curiosity about my weekend activities are totally ignored. In this state of mind facts become overvalued and the search for meaning disintegrates.

What is interesting is that though this more paranoid atmosphere does break the emotional contact between us—my thinking mind disappears, as does hers—we can and do re-establish a more thoughtful and reflective relationship. Sometimes this follows my interpreting, using my countertransference, something of the unbearable nature of her unknowing state of mind and the paranoia it produces; at other times the atmosphere changes for reasons I am not clear about, but which are probably related to my regaining my receptivity to her. This movement in the sessions could be understood as the oscillation between the depressive and the paranoid–schizoid modes of functioning, *in both directions*: movement from the depressive position to the paranoid–schizoid position each time new material emerges relating to unknown matters, and movement from the paranoid–schizoid position to the depressive position as a result of some move towards integration (Britton, 1998).

What the more paranoid interaction does do, though, is fracture the impact of what understanding we may have generated between us—it undermines or breaks links already made or those that are in the process of being made. Mrs F will talk over me or announce that she has not heard a word of what I have said; at other times she says that she goes dizzy, her mind "spinning away". This we came to understand as an attack on the thinking state of mind and the therapeutic process, but the interesting fact is that it is rarely a total attack. The reflective capacity and the therapeutic relationship can be re-established and made further use of, but only in the shadow of likely future disappointment. Suspiciously and carefully watched, it can only ever be partially made use of. Equally, however, often in retrospect, I become aware that the relationship is never totally lost. Some sort of space for thought and reflection is maintained but never allowed to be fully trusted.

I shall return to this patient later, but at this point I will introduce some of the theoretical ideas that I have found useful in my clinical understanding of this and similar patients.

It has been argued that, in a particular way, Bion has significantly developed the psychoanalytic tradition of viewing the Oedipus complex as being at the centre of psychic life.

Bleandonu, for example, in his biography of Wilfred Bion, concludes that Bion "intellectualized" the Oedipus complex. He writes that Bion "transforms the budding Oedipus into someone who is more intellectual than libidinal. . . . Bion inverts the values of the Oedipus complex: the arrogance of seeking to lay bare the truth at any cost overrides murderous sexuality . . . psychoanalysis is devoted to the search for truth" (Bleandonu, 1994).

Symington and Symington write that for Bion, "the mind grows through exposure to truth". Later they say that "Emotional growth has taken the place of sexual libido in Bion's formulation" (Symington & Symington, 1996).

Bion significantly developed a particular strand of the Freud–Klein tradition: his contribution follows both Freud's emphasis on the achievement of insight as being necessary for growth and development ("where id was there shall ego be"), and also Klein's emphasis on the epistemophilic component of the libido, which includes innate knowledge of, for example, the breast, and the penis and vagina and the meeting between the two. In their different ways all three (Freud, Klein, and Bion) emphasize the gaining of knowledge of the self and of the other as being central to psychic health and emotional development.

What Bion has done for psychoanalysis, therefore, is not to abandon the centrality of the oedipal story (which is what I think is suggested in the Symingtons' book) but to emphasize and develop a particular aspect of it. *Coming to know and coming to tolerate the pain of acquiring knowledge are crucial to psychological development.* The question that this raises is how exactly this self-knowledge is achieved and what this knowledge fundamentally consists of.

This leads to a consideration of Bion's concept of "container–contained", which, crucially linked to the notions of "thinking" and "knowledge", refers to an emotional experience originating, in health, in the relationship between mother and infant (Bion, 1962b). The concept of container–contained refers to the maternal provision made available via the mother's reverie to the infant, but the concept is also used to describe a certain aspect of the psychoanalytic process. However, is containment best understood as something that takes place simply in the relationship between infant and mother alone?

I recently came upon the following in Enid Balint's writings that puts my point rather lucidly. In her paper, "Fair Shares and Mutual Concerns", she writes the following: "The quality ... of the object relationship between the mother and the father, as seen and felt by the child in the degree of their capacity to convey mutual concern and fair play, *is a more important introject than the function of either parent taken individually*" (Balint, 1972, p. 68, italics added). Mrs Balint stresses that she is speaking of this experience not only in the oedipal phase of development but in the pre-oedipal period, which involves, for the child, "the beginning of the awareness and the introjection of private and intimate, almost unobservable, collusive, mutually acceptable activities between the parents themselves and between the parents and the child. . . . Once the endurance of this strain has become tolerable to the [child's] ego, there is then the possibility of the development of the idea of fair shares" (Balint, 1972, p. 68).

Enid Balint is talking about the development of the capacity for concern—an emotional capacity comparable to the Kleinian concept of the depressive position. She then overtly expresses her disagreement with writers such as Winnicott, who suggest, she says, that the capacity for concern can be developed in a two-person relationship alone. Her question, she says, is whether this is true or whether "a certain kind of multi-person relationship is also needed. We are now considering a process which starts in the two-person mother–child relationship but needs, if it is to develop fully, *a particular kind of multi-person relationship*, the structure of which has not been described but which deserves serious study" (Balint, 1972, p. 69, italics added).

Britton's paper, "The Missing Link: Parental Sexuality in the Oedipus Complex", written 27 years later, in 1989, addresses precisely this issue so vividly put by Enid Balint. Starting from Klein's views of the early oedipal complex and Bion's concept of container–contained, Britton describes in detail how, if the child is to move towards more mature relating, towards the depressive position, he has to come to tolerate the triangular nature of the oedipal situation. It comes to be seen as truly triangular when the child is able to recognize not only his own relationship to each of his parents, but, in addition, the link between the parents as a couple.

Contemporary psychoanalysis has for some decades now emphasized the *relational* nature of the therapist–patient relationship. Paula Heimann's 1950 paper on the countertransference, based in part on Klein's 1946 delineation of schizoid mechanisms, particularly that of projective identification, dramatically changed our understanding of the nature of the analytic process (Heimann, 1950; Klein, 1946). The fundamental change was to shift the clinical interest away from what was going on inside the patient's mind, to a focus on what was going on in the psychotherapist's mind and in the relationship between patient and therapist.

This is most clearly demonstrated by the clinical emphasis given to the analysis of the transference–countertransference relationship. A deepening understanding has developed of the ways in which the patient, via projective and introjective identification, unconsciously influences the therapist to become involved in and to enact aspects of the patient's internal object relations in the transference–countertransference relationship. As Bion puts it, we find ourselves, "being manipulated so as to play a part, no matter how difficult to recognise, in somebody else's phantasy" (Bion, 1952).

In making this clinical observation, Bion promoted the idea that projective and introjective identification is both an intrapsychic and an interpersonal process. He added to Klein's understanding his view that not only is projective identification an omnipotent phantasy, but the projector unconsciously gives effect to his phantasy by evoking or provoking aspects of that phantasy in the recipient, using verbal and/or non-verbal means. The containing object (initially mother) receives the projection from the other and via her reverie eventually metabolizes it into something manageable and understandable. This is then available for re-introjection by the projector, who not only regains that aspect of himself previously split off and projected, but, crucially, also introjects the experience of containment and specifically the experience of thinking, through which he comes to know himself, and consequently, the world. This process constitutes a potential source of experiential knowledge both about the self and about the other.

This container–contained model has therefore closed the gap between cognition and emotion: gaining knowledge is understood to be fundamentally the result of an emotional interaction. Furthermore, it seems that for Bion the external object is an integral part of the system. Mental understanding by the containing other makes it possible for the individual to develop mental understanding in himself and move towards developing his own mind. (Caper, 1999). As with Klein before him, Bion considers the environment to be crucially important to psychic development, and by using the concepts of projection and introjection he describes the dynamic involved in the mutual interaction between container and contained (Spillius, 1994).

This theoretical development of the container–contained relationship emphasizes the gaining of knowledge as being at the centre of our understanding of psychic development and, therefore, central in the focus of psychoanalytic theory and practice. No longer do we simply think of a patient misperceiving the therapist. We now understand the patient as unconsciously doing things to the therapist—projecting aspects of their internal world into the therapist in a way that affects the therapist. Countertransferentially based experiential knowledge of the patient tends now to be at the heart of clinical practice.

Bion emphasizes the centrality of this process of projective identification to psychic growth and development, be that of an infant or a patient, and particularly at those times when the feelings aroused are felt to be too powerful to be contained within the personality. He says: "Projective identification makes it possible . . . to investigate . . . feelings in a personality powerful enough to contain them." In reality, of course, this process is never quite that smooth, because, on the one hand there may be a disposition in the infant or patient to excessive attacks on and hatred and envy of the object, and, on the other hand, the environment (be that mother or therapist) may not be sufficiently receptive to the projective identifications. Bion goes on to say that "Denial of the use of this mechanism, either by the refusal of the mother to serve as a repository for the infant's feelings, or by the hatred and envy of the patient who cannot allow the mother to exercise this function, leads to a destruction of the link between infant and breast and consequently to a severe disorder of the impulse to be curious on which all learning depends" (Bion, 1959, pp. 106–107).

In his examination of the concept of containment, Britton reminds us that there is a third influence on the containing process between infant and mother—that is, "the identity and personality of the other member of the early oedipal situation, namely the father" (Britton, 1992a). He describes how the father might be either hostile to or solicitous and supportive of the nursing couple, and that this will have a direct influence on both mother and child; but he also stresses that, by identification, the father's attitude can become an internal object capable of either giving aid to or sabotaging the nursing couple (Britton, 1992a). As did Klein and Bion before him, Britton, too, refers to both the constitutional and the environmental factors in the infant/mother/father interaction.

Freud first delineated the Oedipus complex as it manifested itself in the 3- to 5-year-old child with regard to the relationship with the mother and with the father. However, he came to see that the young infant not only wanted to secure the love of the parent of the *opposite* sex, but that this was inevitably pursued with ambivalence because it was felt to be at the expense of an affectionate attachment with the parent of the *same* sex. This dilemma or ambivalence may, in fact, be considered to be nearer to a true understanding of the *triangular* oedipal situation. Though the relationship to mother may be primary, periods of relating to mother *and* to father by infants of both sexes, is probably a more realistic picture of infant development.

Those writers influenced by Klein's clinical work with infants distinguish between the less mature and the more mature forms of the Oedipus complex and so describe the initial anxieties, defences, and object relations relating to the oedipal situation at a more primitive, paranoid–schizoid, level.

Britton has elaborated an additional dimension to the oedipal situation (Britton, 1989) by highlighting that, as well relating to the parents as individuals—as mother and as father—the young child, driven by his natural curiosity, is confronted by the dim recognition of a link between the parents, ultimately their sexual relationship. Later, the child also realizes that there are differences between the relationship of the parents and the relationship between parent and child. Because of the generational difference, the parents may not only exchange physical sexual gratification, but their intercourse may also lead to the actual creation of a new baby. In this process the infant and child is confronted with the pain of acquiring knowledge of the true nature of the parental relationship and of the true reality of the oedipal triangle. If he is to come to tolerate this knowledge and integrate it, he has to relinquish his omnipotence and narcissism. He will have to come to bear "the basic element of human reality: the double difference between the sexes and the generations" (Chasseguet-Smirgel, 1985) and begin to tolerate "the facts of life" (Money-Kyrle, 1968). If this can take place, more mature object relationships begin to be realized.

Britton makes the further point that if the child can tolerate this link between the parents, it provides him with a blueprint for an object relationship of a third kind in which he is witness and not participant. (The first two relationships link the child separately to the mother and to the father.) "A third position then comes into existence from which object relationships can be observed. Given this, we can also envisage *being* observed. This provides us with a capacity for seeing ourselves in interaction with others and for entertaining another point of view whilst retaining our own, for reflecting on ourselves whilst being ourselves" (Britton, 1989).

The development of this capacity for self-reflection (knowledge of the self) and for having the other in mind (knowledge of the other)—clearly achievements of some substantial psychological maturity—constitutes Bion's third factor of psychic life, that which he called "K" or knowledge (Bion, 1962b). By this he meant *not* intellectual knowledge, but knowledge based on experiencing, feeling, and thinking. The other two factors are "L" and "H", love and hate. The integration of the capacity for "K"—for experiential knowing—may be said to be a development of the capacity for containment: a capacity to emotionally manage the likely vicissitudes of human relating, be that the therapist–patient relationship or the parent–child relationship (or the intimate adult couple relationship—see Ruszczynski & Fisher, 1995).

Bion also introduced the notions of "minus-K", whereby from internal sources the infant destroys understanding and learning; and the notion of "no-K", whereby the infant has no (maternal) object available to take in and process his projective identifications. "Minus-K" is understood to be the product of envy and "no-K" to be the product of the lack of a container in the external world through which the infant's mind might develop an apparatus for thinking. Britton has recently offered a suggestion that "minus-K" might be understood not solely in relation to envy but as the product, in part, of an antipathy to knowing anything that is different (Britton, 1998).

Hanna Segal, in a commentary on Britton's paper, suggests that this "triangular space" created as a result of the recognition of the parental link as described by Britton is an *extension* of the original relationship between container and contained as defined by Bion. The *important* difference, she says, is that, "in the original situation the child is a participant and a beneficiary of that relationship. Recognizing the parental couple confronts him with a good contained–container relationship from which he is excluded. It confronts him with separateness and separation as part of the working through of the depressive position" (Segal, 1989).

The development of this sense of the triangular space also offers the opportunity for the infant to begin to learn that there are different types of links and relationships. Some he will always be excluded from, some he will be included in, and some he may create for himself, in his own right, at some future time. The development of this capacity to tolerate this configuration of object-relationships, clearly a capacity of some substantial health—places the individual in the human community.

I would like to suggest that this triangular space as described by Britton, within which the possibility of observing and being observed takes place, is also a more accurate way of understanding the *process of containment*. The third position, from which observation takes place and from which thought eventually emerges, exists in a relationship with the receptive process. It has often been stressed that the container–contained activity, if it is to lead to psychic change, depends on the containing object coming to be able to offer and have accepted not only receptivity but also the insight and knowledge produced by the metabolizing process. Successful containment provides a sense of integration and the experience of being understood, but lasting psychic change does not come automatically from such containment. Containment provides the context for further development to take place, but only with the acquisition of insight and understanding by the patient (Steiner, 1993). Developing an interest in understanding, which reflects the beginning of a capacity to tolerate insight and mental pain, is understood to be associated with a move from the paranoid–schizoid to the depressive position.

The container–contained process requires both the receptivity of the containing object and the object's ability to engage in a reflecting/thinking dialogue within itself, from which emerges an observation or interpretation—this internal activity and the offered interpretation is symbolic of activity other than that engaged in by the infant in being received by the containing object. Symbolically, it may be considered to be the interaction between the female element and the male element that might produce something new as a result of that intercourse. Britton has described how one of his patients, being unable to tolerate him trying to think within himself, screamed at him, "Stop that fucking thinking"—as though she were in the presence of a persecutory couple locked in an intercourse that excluded her (Britton, 1989).

A final point I want to make relates to Segal's comment about the child being a participant and beneficiary of the containing process as is the patient in the psychoanalytic situation. In mother–infant or therapist–patient relationships, the nature of the relationship is necessarily and appropriately asymmetrical, being more for the benefit of the child or patient. Even though such a division of emotional labour will be, from time to time, appropriate within the adult relationship, a healthy adult relationship requires the capacity for symmetry, as there may often be two "equal" claimants for the benefits of the containing process. We could say that this capacity is inherent in the notion of the depressive position. Understanding the nature of adult relationships may, therefore, be significantly aided by adding to Bion's more linear model Britton's notion of the triangular space within which the participant is not only and always a beneficiary of the containment but has to come to tolerate the needs of others who come to be seen as separate objects (Ruszczynski, 1997).

Steiner describes the requirement of mourning the loss of the possessive narcissistic relationship so as to allow for a degree of separateness to take place. He writes that if this can be achieved, "Disowned parts of the self are regained and this ultimately leads to an enrichment of the ego. In the process, however, guilt and mental pain have to be experienced and these may be difficult to bear. If they are bearable the sequence can proceed and further separateness is achieved by progressive withdrawal of projections. More realistic whole-object relationships result . . ." (Steiner, 1990, p. 88).

Mrs F (CONTINUED)

Let me now return to Mrs F. I described earlier the way in which our analytic relationship could be fractured and our capacity to find meaning and understanding be undermined. It was as if we could and did have a thinking space within which we could develop links, but this would then be damaged and lost. This oscillation between a reasonably containing relationship and a breakdown in our emotional contact, between depressive and more paranoid–schizoid anxieties, defences, and object relations, became the main theme of the first two years of our work.

About 18 months into the treatment, Mrs F visited her family home in America and found herself going through her dead father's papers. He had died about ten years previously and so this was not the first time she had done so, but on this occasion, for the first time, she let herself come across and see diaries and letters that showed her that her father had left her and her mother when my patient was about 4 years of age. According to the letters, he stayed away for about a year and then returned.

Mrs F returned to the UK earlier than planned and subsequently returned to the therapy in a state of profound shock. What then emerged was some further understanding of the oedipal situation of her earliest years. As we had already discovered in the transference–countertransference relationship, there could be a—perhaps fragile—reflective space within which there was some capacity for containment and the gaining of understanding. However, this could be fractured and lost, and more paranoid and narcissistic object relations established. Could this be understood to be the result, in part, of the profound fracture in the oedipal triangle when the father disappeared from the family? Undoubtedly the parental receptivity of both parents would also have been flawed as a result of whatever tensions existed before the father's leaving and no doubt on his return too.

As we worked with this material, Mrs F began to refer to her sense of herself being "in a bag with a hole in it"—meaning, we came to understand, that she kept losing her sense of having a skin or boundary: she kept losing her sense of containment. There is a constant "leakage", she would say. But worse than that, she felt that she could not fully trust anyone and had only herself alone to keep "topping up her leaking bag". This seemed a vivid way of describing her oscillation from some capacity to feel contained, which then feels to be punctured and has to be shored up narcissistically.

Mrs F then brought some material to a Monday session that was helpful. She told of three events as if they were one story. The first was of new regulations at the American Embassy and the Passport Office, which meant that the way in which she now had to renew her passport was totally different from the way it had been in the past. For some weeks, she said, she would be without a passport and so would feel herself to be "stateless with no identity". She described herself as the victim of a Kafkaesque situation, where it was not possible to find out what was going on, even though she was being profoundly affected by the change.

She then referred to an argument with her husband over one of their children—an argument for which, she felt, she was partly responsible.

Thirdly, she told me about a dinner party at the weekend when, for no apparent reason, she felt totally excluded and not wanted by the other guests, leaving her feeling isolated, even from her husband. However, during the course of the evening she became aware of there being no reason for these feelings, and she thought that she would bring this experience to her session on Monday. Almost immediately on having that thought, she said, her paranoia disappeared, and she enjoyed the remainder of the party.

I cannot go into the full details of our work with this material, but, in summary, I found myself suggesting that in the course of our separation over the weekend she could find herself in at least three states of mind. The first was the rather Kafkaesque sense of something happening that she had no way of understanding—something that she thought she knew and had available to her was suddenly removed. She was simply a victim of external forces.

The second state of mind was one in which she felt that she had some responsibility for the events taking place, as in her story of the argument with her husband. This had some specific transference implications in relation to a recent discussion we had had about her four sessions being Monday to Thursday, leaving, at her specific request, a three-day weekend.

The third state of mind was more disturbing: something destructive came from within her, as at the weekend dinner party, and she could feel paranoid and rejected even though the external circumstances did not warrant these feelings. She gained relief from this only when she could establish contact with a thinking part of her mind, represented at present by me.

I suggested that this might be a way of beginning to understand what emerges in the therapeutic relationship and no doubt in her real relationships. There could be a sense of a relationship that she takes some responsibility for: that with her husband/therapist. However, this could easily be fractured, and sometimes she felt attacked from outside, by my "Kafkaesque" disappearance at the end of each week, and at other times she felt the impact of powerful forces from within her, which could only be mediated by rediscovering my presence and availability for her.

Just as I was about to finish speaking, my patient suddenly spoke over me and said that she could see patterns in the way my books were arranged in the bookshelves. Immediately she added that she had now gone dizzy and was spinning in her mind and had lost what I had said. "Where are you?" she said. I suggested that for a moment we had perhaps understood some patterns that were worth keeping, like the books in the shelves. But then immediately something dizzy, perhaps even crazy, in her mind spins her away from that insight, and she loses it and also loses her contact with me. Where was I? she had said. In Bion's terms minus-K had come into play, and her dizzy mind attacked possible understanding. However, it is also interesting to wonder whether she became aware that I was about to finish speaking and what she felt terrified by was my impending disappearance, like that of her father concretely, but probably of both her parents in relation to their capacity to keep her sufficiently in their minds. It left her dizzy and spinning.

I think that Mrs F is a good illustration of a patient for whom there is the possibility of movement into the depressive position and its associated anxieties and defences. However, this can also be lost and more primitive anxieties come into play, as a result of which there is a loss of contact with the object, which leaves the patient feeling that her mind is threatened.

Ms B

The second patient I want to briefly discuss is located earlier in the developmental line. Ms B is in her late thirties, is in a stable lesbian relationship of some year's standing, and works, very successfully, as an unqualified architect. I have been seeing her for over three years twice a week, sitting up in a chair. Though it has often come up in the material that two sessions are insufficient, and the possibility of further sessions has been offerred, my attempts to understand this self-deprivation are completely dismissed. Also dismissed is reference to the possible use of the couch: when I interpret something about the couch from her material she very aggressively refuses to consider it and restates rather thoughtlessly that she has no intention of using the couch. To date it has been impossible to understand this beyond vague thoughts of a wish to remain in control.

Bion's notion of no-K, of no available thinking capacity—comes to mind when Ms B is in this totally unavailable state.

When Ms B sought psychotherapy and was referred to me, her father was seriously ill, and he died about six months after we started working together. The most interesting theme in her initial presentation was her bald statement that she wanted to come into psychotherapy primarily because she knew that her father's impending death would be devastating for her, but she was not willing to talk about him and their relationship!

Her other main concerns centred around feelings of frustration and constraint represented most concretely by her having repeatedly delayed, for many years, taking her final professional examinations, even though all her colleagues tell her, and intellectually she herself knows, that she would have no great difficulty in passing these exams. Other concrete areas of constraint and hence frustration included the nature of her social, personal, and sexual life.

Ms B leads an extremely restricted and limited life, tightly controlling all her objects and experiences. "I don't feel jealousy. . . . I don't get angry. . . . I don't see why I need to be aware of ambivalence . . . why should I not idealize my partner or my father . . ."—are the sorts of regular comments she makes. She insists that I have to accept these as truths, and what she finds extremely threatening and persecutory is that sometimes I might have an alternative version of truth or even that I might be curious to understand with her why, for example, she says that she dismisses people who disagree with her by "killing them" in her mind, whilst she goes on claiming never to feel anger or murderousness.

Only much more recently has she allowed herself to consider the possibility that she in fact kills off her feelings and ambitions and that she also feels that I am trying to kill her if I introduce an idea different to hers. Her intolerance of difference is a central theme in the clinical work. I mentioned earlier that Britton has suggested that attacks on thinking may be linked, in part, to an antipathy to knowing anything that is different (Britton, 1998).

It was not possible for a long time for me to have any sense of there being any contact and understanding between us. Any comment or interpretation I made was either totally robbed of any emotional meaning by her intellectualization, or she would very aggressively accuse me of twisting and distorting what she had said and making it unrecognizable. She would subsequently recall these "distortions"—as she called them—and berate me with her protests about them weeks later.

Through my countertransference I came to realize that either I was being totally destroyed by her intellectual responses, which had the effect of a black hole, in that, whatever links I tried to make, she made disappear again, and my sometimes successful attempts to think about my experiences were experienced as violent and persecutory—she attacked and, in her mind, destroyed what I had tried to communicate of my understanding; or, alternatively, whatever I said was experienced as coming from an object that was distorting and perverting her integrity. In other words, the coming together of my thinking about my experience was seen as an act producing something perverse. I often had the experience that Ms B had no internal world of meaning but, rather, managed herself, somewhat anxiously, with her sophisticated intellect, which was at best simplistic and spurious but more often perverse in its clarity and certainty. She seemed willing to sacrifice understanding and knowledge for omniscience.

I want to report two dreams both of which show the nature of her internal world and its object relations and the movement in the psychoanalytic process in the two years or so that separate the two dreams. In the first dream, in the second year of treatment, *Ms B is in a very restricted space with a man whom she is kissing and caressing. She feels a mounting excitement and becomes aware that they are moving towards sexual intercourse. But then, somehow, the space that they are in feels too restricted for intercourse and so instead she finds herself masturbating the man. As she is doing, so the man suddenly changes into a woman, and the penis transforms into two breasts. She continues to stroke and "masturbate" the breasts until each breast "ejaculates" as if it were a penis.* This was all very erotic, she said. When she woke up, she said, she smiled to herself about the dream, but as the day wore on she found herself feeling increasingly disgusted and disturbed by it.

Though my patient could not associate directly to the dream, she said that she was excited and intrigued by the transformation of the man into the woman and the penis into breasts and especially so as neither transformation quite completed itself. Both the initial excitement and then the disgust were, she said, particularly because of these bizarre images.

This dream was useful in that over the next few weeks we were able to use it to consider that in the restricted space of only two sessions of psychotherapy, her intellectualizations were felt to be masturbatory and not the intercourse she actually wished for. The therapeutic container could only be allowed to produce spurious or even perverse contact, about which she could feel perversely excited.

What I could also now say to her with added conviction was how in her mind there could be a very disturbing contact when intercourse is sought which distorts and transforms the experience into something bizarre. Men and women, penis and breast, semen and milk all become confused with each other. Perhaps an alternative to these bizarre and horrifying conjunctions was the killing off of any contact or intercourse via her intellectualization or spurious certainties. I was also able to suggest that the smile at the end of the dream suggested that the perverse part of her smiles in triumph and is in some part pleased with this outcome. As time wore on, however, she could find a state of mind that found it increasingly disturbing.

This dream seemed to prove to be helpful, and there developed a less distorting attack on my comments. What emerged was a fragmented array of belittled, wimpish, disappointing, and stupid men, admirable men (though this was usually the image of her father), and, equally, threatening women, women who had to be protected, and admirable women. Though these figures continued to be part-objects, they were, compared to the figurers depicted in the dream, less splintered and less often joined in bizarre ways.

In the transference I could be any of those figures, sometimes rapidly changing from one into another in the course of a few minutes. Though this produced a very fragmentary experience in the therapeutic process, there was occasionally a possibility of some understanding and meaning being generated. The difference was that any links I might make did not result in bizarre and perverse conjunctions but could very occasionally produce a thought that she could entertain, or sometimes one that even produced understanding.

I had learned that Ms B was brought up by a parental couple who had a very disturbing relationship. Each had a series of affairs throughout her life, but they stayed together mostly because her father was a man of some public stature that neither he nor his wife wanted to threaten with a divorce.

Being the elder of two, she found herself closer to her father, whom she came to idealize consciously. Her mother, feeling threatened by the relationship between father and daughter, was very undermining and dismissive of my patient.

What emerged was a terror in Ms B that there were no constraints or boundaries to her incestuous wishes for her father. There was no sense at all of a parental relationship, and neither was there much sense of a more fundamental container–contained relationship with her mother: her father was seductive and the mother was attacking and dismissive. Emotional contact was, therefore, experienced as perverse or aggressive and attacking. There appears to have been no containing or thinking mind available to her. In Bion's terms, we would refer to no-K. It seemed that Ms B became identified with both the male and female figures, a warring couple in bizarre conjunction.

Something did come to shift for this patient. A dream nearly two years after the one reported previously seems to suggest some struggle towards a sense of ambivalence and the establishing of appropriate generational boundaries.

In this dream, *my patient, not clear whether as a child or as an adult woman, is sitting next to her father. She is stroking his thigh.*

He takes her hand from his thigh and places it on the seat between them. Not deterred, she goes to replace her hand on his thigh, but as she does so, she brushes against his erect penis inside his trousers. She puts her hand on his thigh but freezes with confusion and fear. She thinks that it is not right that her father should be aroused to erection whilst with her. Father then takes her hand off his thigh, places it on the seat between them and holds it down with his own hand.

The work with the dream suggested some clear progress from the previous dream. In this dream there is a suggestion of fragile generational boundaries, though with father and daughter both aroused by each other. Unlike in the previous dream, the figure of the father/man has substance, his existence as the father/man is not in doubt. In addition, there is also a suggestion that the father is determined to try to hold down proper boundaries, even though he might be tempted towards or aroused by my patient. The patient can now hold some thoughts in her mind and establish some thinking space with me, though the seductive pull towards a more incestuous and perverse encounter is ever-present.

* * *

To summarize, then: Bion established the centrality of the container–contained relationship both to the process of psychological development and to the establishment of the capacity for knowledge and self-knowledge. He added the function of Knowledge to those of Love and Hate. He also spelt out the attacks on self-knowledge either from within ("minus-K") or from without ("no-K").

Britton has elaborated the importance of the infant's relationship to the parental couple in this containing process, which, by definition, has to involve an intercourse from which the child is excluded. This brings the role of the father fully into the picture. The capacity to mourn the loss of sole possession of the object and to tolerate observing good intercourse outside oneself is a necessary step towards a more mature capacity for object relating.

The infant's realization and toleration of the link between the sexual parental couple allows for the creation of a triangular space bounded by the three persons of the oedipal situation and all their different relationships. This space provides the arena within which self-reflection, awareness of the other and thought can begin to take place. Out of this there will begin to develop the possibility of a "mind of one's own" (Caper, 1999).

In his observation of and availability to the patient, the psychotherapist is likely to come to know aspects of the patient's internal world and its structures as these are recreated and enacted in the patient's stories and particularly in the transference. In this presentation I have tried to show some of the theoretical ideas that I find useful as I observe my patients and myself in an attempt to contain the bewildering array of experiences they bring to me.